The Very, Very Bad Misadventures of Annika the Reluctant Bookstore Cat

ANNIKA

THE (RELUCTANT) BOOKSTORE CAT

with help from her human servants

Copyright © 2019 Annika the Reluctant Bookstore Cat

All rights reserved

ISBN: 978-1-7331837-0-3

DEDICATION

To myself.

Obviously.

CONTENTS

	Acknowledgements	i
Note about stories 1-8		1
1.	Annika the Spy	3
	Natalie J. Damschroder	
2.	Annika, Guardian of the Enoli	9
	Cathy Leach	
3.	Annika's Christmas	17
	Elizabeth Koerber	
4.	Annika's Chinese Timeout	23
	Jennifer Woodings	
5.	Annika and the Post Office Heist	31
	Jim Fisher	
Note about story 6		41
6.	Rubbed the Wrong Way	43
	Misty Simon	
7.	Foofy McFluffster Saves the Day	51
	Susan Dickinson	
8.	The Princess Tower	57
	Donna L. Leiss	
Note about stories 9-12		65

9.	The Story of My Mysterious Past	67
	Michelle Haring	
10.	I'm the Center of My World	73
	Kristian Beverly	
11.	Queen Annika of the Goblins	79
	Samantha Coons	
12.	Peek-a-boo, Annik-a-boo	89
	Carrie Jacobs	
Content Warning for story 13		**95**
13.	Of Mice and Murder	97
	Odessa Moon	

ACKNOWLEDGEMENTS

I acknowledge no humans.

I suppose I could thank Squeekie for warming up the crowd for the release of my book with his story collections.

And also for being my best friend.

The Very, Very Bad Misadventures of
Annika the Reluctant Bookstore Cat

Note on Stories 1-8

The first eight stories of this collection (and story thirteen) were chosen by a panel of four judges connected to Cupboard Maker Books. The judges were only given the text of the stories, without the titles or any information about the authors. They appear in the order of highest marks given by the judges, with the exception of story thirteen. Due to the violent nature of story thirteen it is placed at the end with a content warning.

We would like to thank all the authors who submitted an Annika story. We received many fantastic stories, but in the end only eight could be included. We are delighted that so many people wanted to help us celebrate Annika, and we hope that you, the readers, enjoy this collection.

Annika the Reluctant Bookstore Cat

1

Annika the Spy

Natalie J. Damschroder

Four feet landing on her table vibrated Annika out of her doze. She blinked and lifted her head slightly. Just Squeekie, not the impertinent kittens. She flicked her tail to show him how unconcerned she was about his presence and laid her head back down.

"The locksmith is done," he told her in a fake-bored voice.

I don't care she told him with her body language.

"You know, the human who had to change the locks because of those guys I saved the store from?"

She yawned.

Squeekie licked his chops. "Yep, Adventure Cat strikes again. You know Mother was very upset at what they could have done. I stopped them."

*What*ever. Annika got up and sauntered to the end of the table, surveying the store's main aisle. Things had been quiet this morning, but she knew that was going to change. There was going to be an Event today, and Mother was very hopeful. The weather was perfect for a crowd inside the store. The crowd would be perfect for Annika. Everyone thought she disappeared during Events because she didn't like humans, but that was simply her very excellent cover. A cover that had never been blown in three years.

The bells bounced on the door, and one of the authors for the Event came in. Annika settled under the table, watching. Squealing voices. Boxes thumping overhead. The human bent to coo at her. She squinted and tensed. But this was one of her people, the few she deigned to allow to pet her. Rising into the stroke, she turned and paused, arching. Then she strode away. Always leave them wanting more.

Within a few minutes, chaos had taken over. Now was the perfect time. Annika padded through the store, making turns to only go down empty aisles. She let herself be glimpsed twice, so the humans would believe she was still present, and when voices faded toward the main counter, she slipped through the tiny gap in the far corner of the back room. A small roll of papers had been hidden just inside the wall. Catching the ribbon holding the roll in her mouth, she made her way inside the wall to the secret opening and pushed the cover outward with her head. It fell back with a tiny bump once she was through.

The sun was slightly beyond its zenith. The Event was starting, and she had plenty of time to reach her rendezvous point and return. A thick cloud darkened the light and removed the warmth of the sun, but that didn't matter. She had a thick coat to keep her warm. Today, anyway. They were making noises about taking her to the groomer for her spring haircut. The "lion" look was *not* her, but she let them have their way in order to maintain her cover. The work she did was very important. Just as important as Mother's fostering of silly kittens and other homeless cats. And it was vital that Annika remain at the bookstore so she could continue that work. She made herself just endearing enough to be kept, but held enough disdain and hostility to keep them from sending her to a new "forever home."

Such were the sacrifices made by the perfect feline spy.

After trotting lightly through the trees and across several yards, she squeezed between fence boards and dashed up unpainted steps onto a porch. After checking carefully for anyone watching, she pawed the flap of a dog door and then sat to wait. A few seconds later, the door opened and she went inside.

Spy cats did *not* use dog doors. Not unless they were compromised. And Annika had never been compromised.

She jumped to the table and dropped the intelligence, licking her chops once to smooth her whiskers.

"Good girl." The man who had opened the door sat in a chair and unrolled the paper. His fingers ruffled the fur at her neck, eliciting a purr as his reward. He grinned at her. "Annika, my pet, you have perfect timing. I need to send something back. But first, your reward." He got up and went to the counter, where a familiar silver bowl sat. He was lucky he gave her top tuna. She was no one's *pet*, and the claim would normally be enough to get his fingers nipped.

But that would be unprofessional.

While she daintily consumed the tuna he placed in front of her, he did something with wires and plastic. Then he fastened a tiny canister to her collar and spun it so it was hidden under her ruff. She licked the last few drops from the bowl and took a few moments to groom.

Partway through washing her face, a loud *boom* from the front of the house made her jump and freeze. The man leaped to his feet, turning to block her from view. "Go," he hissed over his shoulder. She dropped silently to the floor and pressed herself against the wall, crouching to peer between the table legs and see the source of the invasive noise.

Invasive was the correct word. Six legs charged into the front room of the small house. Shouts at her contact were not comprehensible, but they made him raise his hands in the air. A split second later he dove sideways into a roll, coming up with his hands now held in front of him, a dark rod protruding between them. She froze. She knew what that was. Squeekie talked about those noisy, awful things after reading about them in his adventure books. It was a gun. She'd never seen one before, not a real one. It jerked, flame and smoke and the loudest noise she'd ever heard blowing out the end. Her whole body trembled, but she couldn't move. He was in danger. She couldn't leave him. But if she didn't….

He spotted her and frowned. "Go, Annika. Now! You know what you must do!"

She did. The same as she'd always done. Even if it meant….

She whirled and ran with all her considerable speed to the—ick—dog door, pushing through it and racing across the yard, through the fence, between the trees, and back to the small tube that was her secret entrance. Her claws caught the edge of the cover, prying it open, and she ducked her head inside, crawling through into the quiet space.

Then she stood, her sides heaving with her efforts, heart beating so fast it rattled her elegant bones. She let it settle, let her regal calm take over again. There were *things* in her fur, she could feel them. Twigs or leaves, and tiny bits of soil in the pads of her feet. They had to be removed before she went inside the store and made the hand-off. Her exquisite sense of time told her there was just enough left to restore herself before she had to find her final connection. She pulled a twig from her fur with her teeth and carefully erased all evidence that she had been outside. Then she sauntered back through the store, making sure no one saw her until she was near one of her usual drowsing spots.

"There's Annika!" Mother called as she emerged into the main part of the store. "She's such a baby. Hates when we have so many people here."

There were, indeed, a number of humans still surrounding the author table. Annika wound around legs, carefully avoiding touching any. Then one person squatted, hand held out, and she angled over. Acting like a cat, she swiped the side of her face against their fingers, pausing as those fingers curled under her collar and popped off the cylinder.

"Good job, Annika. You will never know the amazing work you've done." A gentle hand swept from her head down to her tail. She snapped it high and walked away, head up. Squeekie watched her from his perch on a bookshelf, and she headed away from him. No more bragging about saving the store. He'd done fine, she supposed, when those bad men came in here. But her connection was wrong. She knew exactly how amazing she was.

Squeekie saved the store. But Annika saved the world.

Annika the Spy

AUTHOR BIOGRAPHY

Natalie J. Damschroder is a multi-published author of contemporary and paranormal romance, with an emphasis on romantic adventure. She also writes YA paranormal adventure as NJ Damschroder. A 2012 recipient of the RWA Service Award and two-time finalist in the EPIC eBook Awards romantic suspense category, she is also a multi-finalist in the International Digital Awards, and the third book in her Goddesses Rising trilogy, *Sunroper*, won the 2014 Prism for Light Paranormal Romance.

Natalie grew up in Massachusetts and loves the New England Patriots more than anything. (Except her family. And writing and reading. And popcorn.) When she's not writing, revising, proofreading, or promoting her work, she works as a freelance project manager. She and her husband have two daughters, one of whom is also a novelist. (The other one prefers math. Smart kid. Practical.) You can learn more about her at www.nataliedamschroder.com or www.njdamschroder.com, where you'll also find links to her blogs and social media.

Annika the Reluctant Bookstore Cat

2

Annika, Guardian of the Enoli

Cathy Leach

From atop the Mystery section, Annika watched Michelle lock the door and head for her car. Cupboard Maker Books had closed for another day. Time to get to work.

"Do you want me to help this time?" asked a voice to her left, giving her a start.

She knew Squeekie, the other resident bookstore cat, would have been happy to help, but Annika would not be satisfied unless she had completed the search personally. After all, it was her responsibility.

"No," she replied, "but, thanks for offering."

She jumped down and headed for a hidden area of the bookstore, a section that even Michelle, the owner, wasn't aware existed.

One by one, Annika examined the books that concealed the portal.

"Sparks, Jordan, Graham, Peretti, Coben," she read aloud. "All present and accounted for."

She returned to the main area and began the search.

Carefully, the cat worked her way over and under each and every shelf and table, checking book titles as she went. The daily ritual took almost three hours and, by the time she finished, Annika was exhausted.

"Find anything?" Squeekie asked.

"Just one this time," Annika answered, "and I took care of it."

"Good," Squeekie said with a nod, then walked off to do whatever it was he did at night. She had no idea because she had never really paid much attention.

With a sigh, Annika shook herself, then settled into her bed to rest. As she dozed off, her thoughts drifted to the past. Back to a time when...

...cats walked upright and her family ruled the territories of Enola.

The land was lush and green, the waters ran clear, and food was plentiful. Life was good and the cat-folk of Enola were happy.

Annika was hardly more than a kitten when her mother, the queen, pulled her aside and shared the news that would change her life. Not only was Annika a member of the royal family, she was predestined to become a Guardian of the Realm.

Serving as a Guardian was a great honor, but it was a difficult status to achieve and could be extremely dangerous. Many of the Chosen couldn't handle the rigorous training process, and those who did were constantly challenged. It was not an easy way of life, but it was necessary.

Not long after Annika's training began, the Enoli received word that an old enemy had resurfaced. He and his army were slowly working their way up from Wormleysburg, gleefully destroying everything in their path.

El Gato del Diablo, the Devil Cat, was aptly named. The huge beast, as evil as Satan himself, took immense pleasure in causing death and destruction everywhere he went. His cruelty was legendary.

After narrowly escaping the demented creature years earlier, the Guardians of Enola devised a plan to stop him if he ever returned.

A local wizard cast a spell over the old cupboard factory, opening portals between two worlds. Between the portals was a passage, filled with darkness and nothing else. If the Guardians could lure El Gato into the passage, it could be locked from both ends, trapping him forever.

Annika, Guardian of the Enoli

Books were the key.

"*That's no way to hold a sword, girl!*"

Angered and, as always, ready with a sharp retort, Annika whirled to face the source of the insult. She glared up into the eyes of the most gorgeous tom she had ever seen. His sleek, black coat drew attention to the small, white crest at his throat. His bright green eyes were flecked with golden highlights.

Her anger vanished instantly, as something like an electric shock ran through her entire body. For a long moment, she could only stand and stare, her mouth gaping open as if she were the village idiot.

"Who are you?" she demanded, when she had recovered her senses enough to speak. "Do you know to whom you speak?"

She spoke with calm assurance, although her insides were churning and she feared he could read her thoughts.

Grinning, the tom removed his hat and, with a sweeping bow, introduced himself.

"I beg pardon, dear princess," he said. "My name is Guntthar. I have been sent from Duncannon to assist in the training of your Guards."

"So, you'll be staying a while," Annika said, hoping she didn't sound as pleased as she felt.

As of that day, training became much more interesting for Annika, and she became Enola's most fearsome warrior. The months passed, and she and Guntthar became very close.

Annika savored the feel of the warm sun on her fur, as she sat with Guntthar in the shade of an old maple tree. The look in his beautiful eyes warmed her almost as much on the inside. Life was good.

"CLANG! CLANG!"

Suddenly, the alarms sounded, breaking the spell.

Annika jumped to her feet. Guntthar grabbed her paw and pulled her with him.

"Come on," he shouted. "We're being attacked!"

"But I'm not ready," Annika protested. "I haven't taken the test."

"You're ready enough," he replied, pausing slightly to give her a reassuring glance.

They ran.

The Captain of the Guard met them as they approached.

"Princess Annika," the guard said, "The king sent me to fetch you. It is El Gato. We must act quickly! Summerdale and Marysville have already fallen."

A chill ran down Annika's back and her heart beat faster than she ever remembered. The moment had finally come.

"Is everything in place?" she asked.

"Yes, Princess Annika. I checked it myself, just this morning."

Giving him a nod of thanks, Annika ran toward the old factory building, Guntthar at her side.

The portal was exactly as it had always been, but Annika thought it seemed different somehow - smaller, maybe, but definitely darker and more menacing.

She shook off the creepy feeling and checked on the books, even though she knew they were all there and in perfect order. Except for one - the last one - the one that would set it all in motion. It lay nearby, ready to be grabbed at a moment's notice.

She knew an identical set of books waited at the other end of the portal.

"Are you sure you want to go through with this?" Guntthar asked softly. "You know it means you can never come back. You'll have to live as an ordinary cat for the rest of your life."

Annika's throat thickened and tears threatened to fall, as she gazed into Guntthar's gold-flecked eyes. She knew she would never see him again. For just the briefest moment, she considered staying. But, no.

"I must do it," she replied firmly. "It's what I was born for."

Through misty eyes, she saw him nod, looking defeated, fighting tears of his own.

Annika, Guardian of the Enoli

They embraced quickly, then Guntthar picked up the book and took his position by the portal. Annika took a deep breath, squared her shoulders, and headed outside to face El Gato.

The street was empty, except for El Gato. He was looking away from her.
The monster was even larger than she'd imagined. And incredibly ugly. His fur was a matted brown mess, his left ear hung loosely to the side, and there was a gaping hole where his right eye had once been. His bulky arms hung almost to the ground and there was something growing from his neck.
Annika shuddered
"Hey, ugly!" she shouted. "Over here!"
He turned his massive head and started toward her.
"C'mon, chicken," she taunted. "I bet you can't catch me."
She reached the doorway to the factory, turning to see him advancing rapidly.
"Sissy!" she yelled, then ran for the portal.
The creature was two steps behind her when she jumped through the opening.

Once inside the passage, Annika saw only darkness. Her heart raced. She thought she might throw up. Her eyes darted back and forth, searching.
"The portal," she cried frantically. "Where is the portal?"
At the precise moment she spied it, only yards away, she heard a furious roar behind her. El Gato was in the passage now and he was not happy.
He banged his mighty fists against the door that had just slammed shut behind him. The door was shrinking rapidly; soon he wouldn't fit through.
His red eyes glowed with the fierceness of his rage. In the darkness, he kicked at the solid black wall that now stood where the opening had been, then, bellowing, rammed it with his shoulder. It had no effect. The doorway was gone.

Annika knew Guntthar had done his part. Now she had to do hers, and quickly. The monster shrieked in frustration, then it turned toward her.

Annika bolted for the portal, knowing she had only a few precious seconds before the beast reached her. She ran for her life.

She felt the monstrous cat's claws brush her tail as she dove through the opening, slammed the door, and jammed the book into the lock slot.

It was done. Again, she heard the creature's screams of rage, as it vainly attempted to crash through the door before it disappeared.

Annika took several deep breaths, waiting for her heartbeat to return to normal. While she recovered, she read the titles of the books that had locked the portals: The Guardian/Trapped/The Evil Inside/Monster/Gone for Good.

She had completed the first part of her mission.

The second part of Annika's mission is to guard the portal. Although the books hold the portal closed, there is one way to reopen it. Another combination of five books, in just the right order, will break the locking spell.

As Guardian, Annika must make sure those books are never allowed in the bookstore, just in case.

Lying on the floor by the vanishing portal, Annika mentally reviewed the authors, then the titles, of the forbidden books, even though she knew them by heart.

"Might as well get started," she said, rising to her feet. She immediately lost her balance and plopped to all fours, blinking in surprise.

"It takes a while to get used to," she heard someone say. "Being a regular cat, I mean."

A Siamese cat stood, on four feet, in the doorway to the bookstore, looking at her curiously.

"I've been expecting you," he said. "My name is Squeekie."

Squeekie watched Annika while she slept. He could tell she was having another bad night. Sometimes she talked in her sleep. Other times, like tonight, she cried, but he would never tell her that.

He knew she missed her Before life, and especially missed Guntthar. She had sacrificed everything in order to save her village. She was a true hero and he was extremely proud of her. Secretly.

Squeekie stroked Annika's back, very gently, so she wouldn't feel it. He hated to see her so sad. It made him sad, too.

He stepped away, picked up the tattered mouse toy he had been chewing earlier, and batted it directly at her face. Bullseye!

"Mrroww!" Annika jumped nearly a foot into the air.

"Squeekie!" she growled. "Just what do you think you're doing? I was sleeping."

"I know," he replied, and walked off, wearing a grin of satisfaction.

"Peasant," Annika grumbled.

"That's better," he said to himself.

Cathy Leach

AUTHOR BIOGRAPHY

Cathy Leach became addicted to reading at an unusually early age and soon moved on to making up stories of her own.

When her daughter was a toddler, Cathy hand-wrote a storybook with colored pencil illustrations and a cover made from a box. "Timmy the Turtle" instantly became a family favorite.

Working for local newspapers gave her an opportunity to write, but she wanted to write fun stories, not just state facts.

Cathy has trained with the Institute of Children's Literature, Writer's Digest, and The Write Practice, among others, and has taken MasterClasses by James Patterson and R.L. Stine.

In 2013, she wrote "Stanley Stinkbug," for the church's talent show. It was a big hit, with an encore reading requested in 2018.

Cathy has had two short stories published online through Short Fiction Break, and her short story, "Strange Summer," was selected for publication in James Patterson MasterClass' second student anthology.

She lives in central PA with her husband and an obscene quantity of books, mostly thriller, suspense, and paranormal. A long list of favorite authors includes Harlan Coben, Linwood Barclay, Preston and Child, and the earlier Stephen King and Dean Koontz.

3

Annika's Christmas

Elizabeth Koerber

It was that time of year again. The days were getting shorter, the weather was getting colder, and in Cupboard Maker Books decorations were being put up for the holiday the humans called Christmas. Squeekie loved the decorations with all their colors and shininess. However Annika was not pleased. She didn't like change, and she thought the whole idea of Christmas was silly.

"I mean, it's completely ridiculous to put a tree inside!" she complained to Squeekie one day. "Even a fake tree looks out of place."

"I think it's nice," Squeekie said. "Humans talk about peace and love around this time of year. And that includes love for animals."

"There's nothing stopping them from talking about peace and love at other times of the year," Annika said grumpily. "You don't need a whole holiday just for that.

"It's not just about that," Squeekie pointed out. "I love the Christmas season. I think my favorite part is Santa Claus. He brings toys to good kids, and maybe he'll bring some treats for good cats too."

Annika rolled her eyes. "Come on, Squeekie. Santa isn't real! Humans made him up because he's a fun thing for their kids."

Squeekie looked shocked. "Santa Claus IS real!" he insisted. "There are all sorts of pictures of him and stories about him. How can Santa be made up when all that stuff that exists?"

Annika snorted. "Just because there are stories and pictures doesn't mean something is real. After all, there are lots of fantasy stories in this store about unicorns, and they don't exist either."

"They don't?" Squeekie asked sadly.

Annika just sighed. "You can believe if you want, but trust me. Santa Claus is not real. And even if he was real he couldn't bring treats to us. The stories all say he comes down the chimney. We don't have a chimney."

Squeekie looked very sad.

The days passed and Christmas got closer and closer. People coming into the shop talked about buying gifts for themselves and other people. The kids in the store talked about Santa Claus. Squeekie followed them around, eagerly listening to the stories. Annika, as usual, ignored everyone.

Finally Christmas Eve rolled around. Squeekie still fully believed in Santa Claus. "I'm going to stay up tonight and see Santa visit the store," he told Annika proudly.

Annika just shook her head. "You can do that if you want. It's your time to waste."

When the bookstore closed Squeekie settled himself in his favorite bed and resolved to stay awake all night watching out the windows. Annika retreated to her own bed and promptly closed her eyes, ready for a good night's sleep.

Although Squeekie tried his hardest to stay awake he could feel his eyelids beginning to droop as the night continued. Finally his eyes closed, and he drifted off. Annika had been sound asleep for several hours by then.

A little while after Squeekie fell asleep the door of the store creaked open very slowly. A stranger was quietly making their way into the shop.

Annika roused herself from sleep when she heard the door open. She was confused. There shouldn't be any humans in the shop right now. Not only was it a holiday, but it was the middle of the night. She realized it must be a thief. She quietly got up and crept toward the door. She would deal with anyone who dared to steal from her shop!

Annika's Christmas

Annika reached the door pretty quickly, and got ready to pounce on the thief. She puffed out her fur and let out a growl.

Before she could attack the stranger spoke. "Annika, please don't growl at me. It's not nice."

Annika was shocked and stopped in her tracks. She took a good look at the stranger. Standing in front of her was a man dressed in black boots and a red fur suit with white trim. He had white hair and a white beard, and he carried a large bag. He also had on a hat that matched the suit. "That's impossible!" Annika whispered to herself.

To her surprise Santa Claus answered her. "Why is it impossible, Annika? You can clearly see I'm right here."

The response threw Annika for a loop. "You understand me?"

Santa smiled. "I'm a magical being. Part of that magic is speaking to animals. It would be pretty hard to tell my reindeer where to go if I couldn't communicate with them." He motioned out the door where a sleigh and reindeer were standing in the parking lot. "Another part of my magic is traveling all over the world in one night."

Annika took this all in for a minute then asked another question. "But why are you here? This isn't a house; this is a store. We don't even have a chimney."

"I don't always need to use a chimney. I can get inside many different ways. And I'm here because your friend Squeekie was right," Santa Claus explained. "I don't just bring treats and toys for good human children but for cats and other animals as well." He reached back into his sack. "In fact, I have a nice tuna treat for both you and Squeekie."

Annika perked up. "For me too?"

Santa smiled kindly. "Yes, for you too Annika. You don't warm up to people like Squeekie does, but overall you're still a good cat. You can't help being a bit grumpy naturally."

Annika felt immensely pleased at this. Then she thought of something. "Let me go get Squeekie! He'll be thrilled to see you're real. He always believed. In fact, he was trying to stay up tonight to watch for you. I guess he fell asleep though."

Santa Claus nodded. "That's part of my magic too. I only come when everyone is asleep."

Annika frowned in confusion. "Then why am I awake?"

"Although it is best to make my stops when everyone is asleep I can wake some people – and animals – if I feel they need a dose of the Christmas spirit. You needed to see me, Annika. You're generally a good cat, but you shouldn't be so bothered by the Christmas season. Even if it causes changes in the store. It only comes once a year. Try not to let your natural grumpy tendencies make you forget the message of Christmas. Peace on earth and goodwill towards all living things. That also means you should try to be nicer to the people here. They love you."

Annika frowned. "I'll try not to be so bothered. And I suppose I could... try to be nicer. But I don't have to let people touch me or pick me up do I?" She shuddered at the thought.

Santa smiled at Annika. "Just try," was all he said. Then he reached into his bag and pulled out two small tuna treats. There was one for Squeekie and one for Annika. Santa set them on the floor. Then he gathered up his bag and went back out to the door. "Merry Christmas, Annika," he told her as he stepped out to his sleigh.

Annika was tired so she went back to her bed and slept long and hard for the rest of the night. The next morning when she woke up she wondered why she had dreamed about meeting Santa Claus in the middle of the night. *"What a strange dream,"* she thought. Then she heard Squeekie yelling.

"Annika! Annika! Santa came last night! Come see what he left us."

Annika walked over to where Squeekie was waiting for her, and was jolted by the sight of two small tuna treats exactly where Santa had left them in her dream. She realized that meeting Santa must have been real and not a dream at all.

"Isn't this great?" asked Squeekie as he started to eat the tuna. "Santa left us a wonderful gift!" Then he paused. "Sorry Annika, I forgot. You don't believe in Santa. Maybe the humans who work here snuck in and left this for us."

Annika shook her head. "No Squeekie, you were right the first time. I think Santa left this for us."

Squeekie's eyes widened. "What changed your mind?"

"I think I just got a dose of Christmas spirit," Annika replied.

Squeekie didn't quite understand what Annika meant by that, but he was too happy to wonder about it. "Merry Christmas, Annika."

"Merry Christmas, Squeekie."

Elizabeth Koerber

AUTHOR BIOGRAPHY

Although **Elizabeth** has enjoyed writing all her life and has written many stories, this is her first published work. She also enjoys reading and reads about 100 books per year. Her favorite genre to both write and read is fantasy. In addition to reading and writing she spends her time singing with the Harrisburg Choral Society and volunteering at her local library. She has a bachelor's degree in French and a Master of Science degree in Library and Information Science. Elizabeth went to school in Virginia and Tennessee. She then lived in Georgia before returning to Central Pennsylvania. She lives with her mother, who she takes care of. She is a huge cat lover so she also has two extremely spoiled cats.

4

Annika's Chinese Timeout

Jennifer Woodings

Legends say that in the beginning the Unknowable placed Cats in charge of all creation. The Cats preferred to enjoy the pleasures of the world and suggested that Mankind would be better suited to this task. So the Unknowable settled for making Cats the keepers of time. To this day you can hear the machinery that moves the world through the heavens within their purr.

Another day in the bookstore had come to an end. As usual, several of the regular humans had hung around until far later than Annika would have liked. After the last one had straggled their way out into the darkness Annika emerged from her well-chosen hiding spot. She watched as Squeekie stalked off to do his standard night watchman routine. The two newest rescues had curled up in a ball together, exhausted after the excitement of meeting so many new people. The thought of so many people handling her made the ball of fluff at the tip of Annika's tail swish back and forth. Unlike a dog, she didn't need to fawn over the merest bit of attention the humans would give her. It was shameful the way the other cats would purr at the drop of a feather. Some of them all it took was for a human to say their name.

"Has no one taught these overdeveloped apes to look with their eyes and not with their hands?" the Himalayan thought to herself as she hopped down from the counter and wandered toward the large window at the front of the store. "And do none of them have the good taste not to draw attention to a bad haircut? I mean, it's obvious they're terrible at maintaining their own fur with as little as they're able to keep on their bodies, so really who are they to judge?" Bars of light crossed the floor in front of her as cars drove by outside. A single graceful leap deposited her on the table top where she settled down to groom herself, trying to make the best of her new haircut.

His inspection of the back room finished, Squeekie ran up the ramp to the catwalks. The rattle of the catwalk's bouncing behind him echoed through the empty store. Annika paused to glare at him then returned to her grooming with a single irritated flick of her ear. The Siamese patrolled along the catwalk on silent paws, pausing here and there to stare down at the tops of the bookcases. Satisfied, he trotted to the end of the catwalk where it overlooked the front window and settled himself down with his paws tucked beneath him.

"You know," he mused, "I think you look great. The absolute peak of feline fashion, sporting those boots with the fur." He peered down at Annika only to see that she had turned to work on her back legs, conveniently placing her back toward him. "Oh come on! That was funny and you know it," he protested as he sat up. "Everyone who came in today said you looked beautiful, I don't understand why you're so upset."

"Of course not," she snapped back between licks, "you've never had to suffer this indignity yourself."

Squeekie thought for a moment then turned, sauntered back across the catwalk and leapt down to the floor. With purposeful strides he crossed the floor and ducked under the curtain into the little back room where his young human spent his time. "I know just what you need, Annika. Now I know I saw some back here somewhere," his voice trailed off amidst the sound of crinkling plastic bags. "Ah! There it is." With gentle teeth he picked up the small plastic wrapped cookie and carried it out to deposit it on the table in front of his friend. "Here, the humans call these 'Fortune Cookies' and the little slips of paper in them seem to make them happy. This ought to put a purr in your chest. "

"I know what a fortune cookie is, Squeekie. I'm not one of the kittens," Annika grumped as she batted the cookie between her paws. "A silly slip of paper isn't going to fix this disaster, though. Only time can. And it certainly won't make me purr, I'm not so easy to charm." With a derisive sniff she swatted the cookie away from her and onto the floor. Then she curled up in the cat bed closing her eyes as if she were sleeping.

Squeekie moved to lay next to her then thought better of it. "Ok Annika. When you want to talk, you know where to find me."

Once she was sure that he was gone, Annika opened her eyes and stretched. She had thought watching the train yard would relax her but more and more she felt like she was on display. As she turned from the window to seek out another place to sleep she was startled to find herself with Squeekie's butt in her face. "Squeekie! What do you think you're doing," she chastised as she sat back with a thump. It was at that moment that she realized that he was floating in midair. "Wait. How are you doing that?" Annika stepped forward and tapped Squeekie's hip with first one paw, then the other. But he didn't reply, not even a whisker twitched. The puzzled Himalayan leapt to the floor to inspect her floating friend from another angle. Sitting back on her hind legs she stretched a paw up and poked Squeekie on the nose and still got no response. "Squeekie? This isn't funny."

"No, it isn't Annika. It's quite serious," a voice Annika didn't recognize stated. It sounded like it was coming from up on the table, but the light shining in through the window made it hard for her to see.

"Who's there," Annika challenged, puffing herself up to look her most imposing. "What did you do to Squeekie?"

From the light glaring off the table top emerged a pure white Persian. "I am Li Shou, and I did nothing to your friend," she replied, her leap to the floor landing her silently next to Annika. "If you're looking for the source of your friend's condition you would do well to look in a mirror."

Annika glared into the strange cat's eyes, noticing as she did that one was a brilliant copper and the other a deep blue. Something in those eyes made her wary and comforted at the same time. It was a confusing sensation that caused her to drop her gaze and relax her posture. "Well, whoever you are, I don't know how I could be the one responsible for this. I didn't even do anything. Who are you to come in here all high and mighty and accuse me of … I don't even know what?"

"As I stated before, my name is Li Shou. And the fact that you, 'didn't even do anything,' is exactly why you're responsible for his condition. You have forgotten your responsibility, Annika."

"My responsibility? I'm a cat, I have no responsibilities. I do as I please," she replied with a haughty sniff. As she spoke the elegant Persian's ear flicked sideways. "I'm talking to you, pay attention."

"Oh, I am paying attention. More so than you. Do you hear that?" Li Shou nodded in the direction her ear had flicked. "Of course you don't, there isn't anything to hear now. Come, I'll show you." The Persian glided up to the indignant Himalayan, and grasping her by the scruff of the neck, led her away. With a leap the two cats moved in a blink from one end of the store to the other where they stopped in front of a clock. Letting go of Annika's scruff Li Shou sat back on her back legs and tapped the front of the clock with a single extended claw. "Now do you see?"

Annika gave herself a little shake to resettle her fur before answering, "I see a clock. What's the big deal?" Faster than she would have thought possible Li Shou's other paw flicked out and tapped her between the eyes causing them to cross for a moment.

"How self-absorbed can you be, child? Listen, and watch. Tell me what is missing."

Startled by the intensity of the other cat Annika blinked then stared at the clock. Her ears twitched side to side trying to figure out what the other cat was so determined to make her notice. The stillness of the dark store around them taunted her. "This is the longest second I've ever spent staring at a clock, Li Shou. Just tell me…" she trailed off, sudden realization dawning upon her. "The clock isn't ticking, the hands aren't moving." She craned her head a little closer to the clock face, "The batteries must have died. But I didn't know it could stop between seconds."

"Almost like it's frozen, isn't it," Li Shou prompted.

Annika stared at the Persian, careful not to meet those unnerving eyes. "Do you really expect me to believe that time has frozen? Assuming I were to believe such a silly notion, wouldn't I be frozen too? It just strains belief." Now that she had noticed it though she couldn't stop hearing the unnatural silence of the store. The little sounds her mind had learned to filter out were now missing in truth. A chill rippled down her spine. Time couldn't freeze, could it?

"Yes. Time can be frozen, Annika. Right now, it has only frozen within this store. But it could spread to the whole world if left unchecked."

Annika rubbed a paw across one ear and then the other. The unnatural silence made them feel funny. "Okay, so fix it," she replied, "Everything was fine until you showed up, so I don't see why this should be my responsibility."

Li Shou growled and cuffed Annika on the side of the head. "I would if I could, but only the one who brought this to be can reverse it. You are responsible because it is your lack of action that caused this. Tell me, child, when was the last time you purred?"

"I'm not a child! And that is no body's business but my own," Annika hissed at the Persian. "I purr when it suits me and that's all you need to know."

"You don't know who I am, do you? Do you know nothing of your own history? I am Li Shou, and I have watched over our kind for ages uncounted. It was I who ensured that Cats would be free to enjoy the pleasures of the world. But that freedom did have a price, we must keep the clockworks of the world wound with our purrs. If we fail to do so, time ceases to pass and brings an end to our pleasure. So I ask you again, child, when was the last time you purred?"

As the Persian spoke she seemed to grow larger than any cat Annika had ever seen before. The white fur seemed lit from within and sparks danced across its tips. Without thinking Annika flattened her ears, crouching low before Li Shou's wrathful form. "Forgive me, Li Shou," she whispered, "I didn't know. It has been too long since I purred, but I haven't had anything to purr about for a long time." The fear in her eyes softened into a wistful gaze.

The Persian leaned forward and gave Annika's forehead a gentle comforting lick. "I know all about your life, it's not necessary for you to speak about the past. But, in wishing for the joys that have passed you have been missing out on the joys still to come.

There is nothing wrong with missing things that are gone, but we cannot live in the past. The past is already gone and by trying to reclaim it you have stopped moving forward." Li Shou settled herself companionably next to Annika. "Why do you insist there is nothing to purr about here? You are a virtual queen of your domain. Innumerable humans gaze upon you daily and lavish you with praise, yet you shun them and take no joy from it."

Annika hung her head for a moment thinking about the Persian's words. "But they also give me this ridiculous haircut and then mock me for it. Even Squeekie mocks me for the furry boots I'm forced to wear."

The Persian's head lifted in confusion. "Oh, Annika is that all you can see? When they give you this haircut, don't you feel so much more comfortable as the weather gets warmer? Doesn't your coat grow back soft and full as the weather gets cooler?"

"I suppose that's all true," she allowed, "and it does make it easier for me to manage by myself. When you put it that way, it doesn't seem so bad. I do get more treats after my haircut too."

Li Shou remained silent and watched as Annika began to rethink her view of life in the bookstore. She could almost hear the gears turning in the Himalayan's mind as her view was remade. Pictures changed from annoyances to badges of honor. The seasonal haircut became seasonal fashion instead of a comical costume. A stable home with loving humans, while other cats have come and gone. Things taken for granted being seen in a whole new light. The Persian could feel Annika relaxing as she began to realize everything joyful in her life.

The second hand ticked.

Li Shou leaned into Annika's side, feeling more than hearing the rusty rumble deep within the Himalayan's chest. Both cats blinked slowly and gently butted heads. The night sounds of the bookstore wrapped around them like an old familiar blanket. They watched for a minute as the hands of the clock counted the passage of time once again. Li Shou grinned.

When the store opened the next morning Michelle noticed the fortune cookie laying in the middle of the floor. Not wanting it to go to waste she opened it and on the little slip of paper inside it said, "It's time to get moving. Your spirits will lift accordingly."

Jennifer Woodings

AUTHOR BIOGRAPHY

Annika's Chinese Timeout is **Jennifer's** second published short story. Her first short story, Squeekie and the Goddess, can be found in the short story collection The Second and Third Nine Lives of Squeekie the Bookstore Cat. She studied English Writing at Edinboro University but was forced to stop when she was diagnosed with a rare lung disease called Lymphangioleiomyomatosis (LAM). A self-described perfectionist and procrastinator, she knows that someday she's going to be awesome. In the meantime, she's in the process of starting a blog about books and her journey with LAM.

Visit her blog at http://fromthebibliophilesattic.blogspot.com
Learn more about LAM at https://www.thelamfoundation.org/

5

Annika and the Post Office Heist

Jim Fisher

Cupboard Maker Books — Evening

Nudge.
Nudge, nudge, nudge.
"Annika? Annika, are you awake?"
Well, I *was* taking a nap. Emphasis on "was."
"I am now, Squeekie. Stop nudging me. What do you want?" Maybe I was a little cranky, but aren't you when you were in the middle of a nice nap and someone wakes you up? Although, looking around, it was dark in the store and nobody was here, so maybe it was more than just a nap. Rain pelted the windows, and lightning occasionally brightened the outside. I grimaced at that, but turned my attention back to Squeekie.

"There's a problem, Annika, and we need to fix it!" Squeekie was more excited than usual, so I suppose he was worried. I stretched, spreading out my toes and arching my back. I made a big show of it, so he knew I didn't have the same degree of worry. Then I yawned, sat down, and began to groom myself.

I looked up from my grooming to see Squeekie sitting there, shifting his weight back and forth on his front paws. I paused in my grooming for a moment. "Okay, what is this problem?" To be honest, I expected it to be something simple, something that isn't a problem in reality. I wasn't far wrong.

"You know that party they are having here tomorrow? The one everyone decorated for today?" I looked around the bookstore.

Banners hung in the darkness, and they'd set up a special table, but it had nothing on it. That was curious.

"I'm aware of something going on, yes. I'd rather everyone just left me alone, though. What about it?" I returned to my important grooming work.

"The book! The book isn't here! I heard the people say something about it still being at the…um…'post office,' I think they called it. It's coming from somewhere called the 'printer,' is what they said. It needs to be here for the party tomorrow! We need to go get it!" Squeekie jumped up, ready to go to this "post office" right away.

"Squeekie, I don't understand how that's our problem. That's a problem for the people." I started to settle down again, intent on going back to sleep.

"But Annika, the book is about you! That's what the party is for!" Squeekie nudged me again, a little harder this time. I sat up and stared at him until he stopped fidgeting.

"About me, you say?"

Squeekie nodded.

"And the party is for the book? Not me?"

A shake of the head.

"I won't be bothered, but people will still celebrate me?"

A vigorous nod.

I thought for a moment.

"Alright, Squeekie. Let's find this post office."

Cupboard Maker Books — later that evening

Getting out of the bookstore was easy enough. We knew how, we just didn't want to most days. I'm not going to tell you how we get in and out. A cat has to keep *some* secrets, after all.

It was still raining when we got outside — a slow, soaking rain. I shook my fur to get the worst of the wetness out, but it was no good. The water soaked right back in again. I glared at Squeekie. *This had better be good,* I thought.

Despite the weather, workers were repairing the road in front of the store. They stopped traffic, only letting the cars from one direction go at a time, before allowing the cars from the other direction to go. The people waving at the cars had water dripping from their hats and clothes. I knew how they felt, and I'd only been outside for a little while. Still, we had a job to do. Looking up and down the line of cars and trucks, I saw one with a familiar symbol on it.

"Squeekie, look! Isn't that the same symbol that the mailperson wears?" Squeekie chirped agreement. "Then it might go to this post office place. Let's go, and get this done. I'm already wet, and miserable, and I want to go back to sleep."

We dashed to the truck without anyone seeing us. We are cats, after all. That sort of thing comes naturally. However, we didn't see anywhere to sit, and the driver was so high off the ground. He couldn't see us anyway. As we explored around the truck trying to find somewhere to hop on, it made a loud noise and started to move. Our time was running out!

In desperation, I ran toward the front, thinking that maybe I could draw the man's attention, and he'd let us in where he was, where it was warm and dry. While that didn't work, I did see a spot to sit. It would be miserable, but it would work.

"Squeekie! Jump up here!" To show him where to go, I made a running jump to a space behind where the driver sat, in front of a big box the truck pulled behind it. Squeekie jumped up with me, and we settled in as best we could. Water splashed up from the truck's wheels, and it was still raining, so yes, it was miserable.

The truck got through the work area and picked up speed. Water sprayed on us harder, and my fur was soaked and matted to my skin. I started to growl, low in my throat, but then the truck turned, and then went faster still. We had to hold on where we could, jamming our bodies into crevices so we wouldn't fall. Falling from the truck would be an awful end to the day. I stared hard at Squeekie.

"Squeekie, I hope this truck takes us where we want to go. It will be very bad otherwise."

Even over the sound of the truck, and the road, and the other cars on the road, I could hear Squeekie gulp.

Post Office — Night

The trip felt like forever. Water splashed up on us from the road. Water fell on us from the sky. Water dripped on us from the truck. The truck's bounces, turns, and movement made us cling on for dear nine lives. We arrived somewhere bright, with what seemed to be a lot of activity. The truck stopped, and then moved backward. It slowed, turned a little, and went backwards again. This time, it bumped into something and came to a complete halt.

When it was over, I jumped down from the truck and bolted for the first place under cover I could find. I was hoping to find a dry place to give myself a quick groom, but there was nothing. Everything was too wet. I sprinted from place to place, desperate to find somewhere, anywhere, so I could groom, but I found nothing at all.

Squeekie ran to me, yelling as he went, and pulled me from my near panic.

"Annika! We have to find the book and get back! It's late now!"

He was right. As much as I hated the thought of another ride like the one we just finished, we were here, the book was inside, and we needed to get this done. *The sooner we get the book, the sooner we get back and I get some* real *sleep.*

The first problem was how to get inside the building. With a line of closed doors and a number of large trucks, the task seemed impossible. Just then, I heard a metallic squealing noise, and saw a shaft of light spill out into the rainy night. Someone had opened a door! The downside was that it was the door behind our truck, and it was even higher than where we'd hitched a ride. That was hard enough — how were we going to get up that high to get in?

Squeekie nudged me again, and pointed. To the right of the door stood a small pile of wood. It was easy for us to scamper up the pile and make the leap to the truck. Don't let Squeekie tell you I slipped while landing. I deny everything.

Once on the truck, we ducked as a large metal cart clanged overhead. The driver pulled it into the building, full of boxes of various sizes. I longed to sort through them in the hopes at least one would be empty, but we had a job to do. Still, I will say that I will never understand humans. They get a box sent to their house, open the box, take the thing that's inside, and throw away the box. Why? The box is the best part! Although sometimes they give it to me, and boxes make ideal places for naps…

I digress.

Back to the action at hand. Squeekie and I slunk out of the truck, and what we saw made us stop in our tracks. Machines of all shapes and sizes pushed envelopes, bags, boxes, and more through a maze of moving belts. Some of the boxes came to rest in large carts that looked like laundry hampers. I don't understand the significance of all of it, but I'm sure it all does what it's supposed to do. Except, in our case, in not enough time.

And the noise! Between the machines themselves, some of the people driving machines on wheels, envelopes fluttering as the machines sorted them, boxes banging against the walls of the moving belts, and people talking, it was almost too much to take in.

We found refuge under one of the belts, and we hid there for a moment to plan our next move.

"Where do you think the book is?" Squeekie asked.

"I'm not sure, but it probably isn't in one of those envelopes." I nodded in the direction of a cart filled with trays. Each tray was full of envelopes, all of which were small and flat. "The books at the store are all bigger than that, right? It would need to be a bigger package, like a box."

Squeekie nodded vigorously. "So we need to go to where the boxes are, right?"

"Right you are, Squeekie. Let's find out where the boxes go."

We snuck out from our hiding place, and had to jump right back into it as a worker drove past us on one of those little car-like things a few people were driving around the building. He didn't even stop to check how we were. He just kept going, without seeing us. We ducked and dodged between machines, getting underneath them where the people couldn't go. We wanted to get on top of them, both so we could see, and because as cats, we like to be up high so we can survey our territory. It was unnerving to have to slink underneath the machines, where it was dirty and dark, to get to where we were going. It was small and not at all like a nice, comfortable box under there as well.

Even with those difficulties, we followed the louder banging noises until we found a massive machine. Moveable walls divided ramps, chutes, and moving belts, transporting boxes from a central point at the end of the machine, to wheeled hampers placed at various points around the machine. Boxes moved along the belts until they got to the ramps, at which point a person would look at each box and push it to where it went. All we had to do was find one box in all of these carts. Easy, right?

Wrong.

We nearly got caught two or three times, digging through hampers trying to find the right box. This one was too big, that one was too small. This box is too heavy, that box is…oh. That box is perfect. The exact size, shape, and weight for a book. I chewed a hole in the box and looked. There was a book in there, but I couldn't see a picture of me on the cover. I saw a picture of a ship with a black flag at the top. That definitely wasn't it.

We searched through more hampers, getting more and more tired as we went. At that point, I'd chewed holes in a dozen boxes, and Squeekie chewed a few as well. We hopped into one last hamper. It doesn't have a lot in it — barely enough to cover the floor — but we looked, just to be sure.

Five boxes into our search, we found another perfect candidate. I chewed a hole in the box to see what was in there, and I saw a somewhat familiar face looking back at me. There I was, looking back at myself.

"Squeekie, come here, I found it," I called.

He bounded over and helped me chew a bigger hole in the box so we could extract the book. Once we did, I reached in and snaked the book out through the opening. It was a lucky thing that it was just small enough that I could grab it in my mouth and carry it without too much difficulty. I don't know what I would have done if it had been bigger.

As we climbed out of the hamper, we saw a large man in a blue uniform point at us, upset.

"Rhmun!" I yelled to Squeekie, or tried to, with the book in my mouth. I meant, "run," and Squeekie must have understood me because that's what he did.

We both took off, in opposite directions, with different yelling people close behind. It was harder for me, since I couldn't go underneath the machines with the book in my mouth. I had to stay in the aisles, or jump up on the machines themselves. I didn't know how those machines work, or what was supposed to move, so I stayed down low and ran as fast as I could.

Even though the people were big, clumsy (compared to cats), and not all that smart, sorry to say, they knew their workplace. They nearly cornered me twice. The only thing that saved me was my speed. What can I say? Four feet are better than two are, I suppose.

Still, they couldn't catch us, and after a few more minutes of chasing, they determined that they must have chased us out. Which was, after a fashion, true, but only because we had to get back to the store with the book.

I won't bore you with the details on how we got back to the bookstore. It was similar to how we got to the post office in the first place, but wetter, and colder. It was worse for me, as I sat on the book to keep it from flying away on the trip back. Suffice to say that we did catch a ride back to our home, and we brought the book with us as well.

Cupboard Maker Books — the next morning

Nudge.
Nudge, nudge, nudge.
"Annika, wake up! The party's about to start!"

I groan. I didn't get enough sleep after our adventure last night. Of course, I couldn't go to sleep with wet, matted fur — so I had to stay up later, grooming myself, before I could go to sleep. So I got that much less sleep than Squeekie did.

"What, Squeekie? We got the book back, they're going to have their party, and you and I are the big heroes. What more is there with which to concern ourselves?"

"Oh, nothing. I just wanted to tell you everything is great! Um...most everything, anyway. The book is wet, though, and they say they're mad at the post office for that." Squeekie sat with his head down, as if he worked for the post office himself, and it was entirely his fault.

"Squeekie, listen — we got the book here. They have a book, and it's the right one! They need to be happy with that. If they can't...well, that's not my problem." Again, I began to settle back in, hoping Squeekie would have learned to take a hint.

I was wrong. Again.

His worried pacing got on my nerves quickly.

"Squeekie?"

"Yes, Annika?" The pacing stopped, and for that, I was glad.

"Will it make you feel better and take your mind off things if I join you at this party?" I said through gritted teeth.

Oh! That would be great!" Squeekie was nearly beside himself with happiness. Reluctantly, I got up, looked at the party, and steeled myself for interactions with people. I sighed.

"Yeah. Life of the party, that's who I am. Let's get this over with, Squeekie." With that, a pair of tired, still damp, but otherwise satisfied cats joined the party.

Annika and the Post Office Heist

AUTHOR BIOGRAPHY

Jim Fisher is a part-time writer, hopping from project to project as he can. He's mostly produced content in the role-playing game industry, having contributed to games such as **Werewolf: the Forsaken**, **Demon: the Descent**, and **Promethean: the Created** for Onyx Path Publishing (amongst others). He also dabbles in local community theatre, where he acts, does light design, set construction, and pretty much anything else that needs done. Finally, he'd like to thank his awesome friend and fellow contributor Susan for challenging him to this contest, and Cupboard Maker Books for sponsoring the contest in the first place. Oh, and also Annika, of course!

Annika the Reluctant Bookstore Cat

*The Very, Very Bad Misadventures of
Annika the Reluctant Bookstore Cat*

Note on Story 6

"Rubbed the Wrong Way" is based on a Mind Mapping session held at the Cupboard Maker Books and led by Misty Simon on March 23, 2019. Eight people came to this workshop. The participants were Teresa Peschel (aka Odessa Moon), Donna L. Leiss, Jennifer Woodings, Dana Armstrong, Bill Peschel, Cathy Leach, Carrie Jacobs, and Nellie Batz. Annika would like to extend her thanks to those that helped create the mind map for this story.

Annika the Reluctant Bookstore Cat

6

Rubbed the Wrong Way

Misty Simon

It had been five days since I'd asked Squeekie to help me with an issue we were having at Cupboard Maker Books. We both lived here full time, and I believed that it was up to us to take care of things around the old homestead. But in five days that cat had done nothing. I'd asked nicely, or as nicely as I did anything, which might have meant I'd yowled loudly at him to get his rear end in gear, but he knew I meant well.

And yet he'd done nothing, just wore his ridiculous bow ties and sashayed around the store taking Michelle paintbrushes from the back. She didn't need them, but she was nice enough to thank him every time he brought yet another one out. I, on the other hand, often told him she didn't need his random gifts. Especially now, when we had a real problem. A real problem of the worst kind. A real problem of epic proportions that made life around here tough, and I didn't like tough.

Books were going missing, and in a bookstore that was the worst kind of trouble to have.

Personally, I thought the culprits were the mice, with their dark fur and beady little eyes and long teeth in the front. I disliked them intensely. They scampered all over the place and chewed through things. It was our job as the store cats to keep them away from the thousands of books on our shelves. Or at least that was supposed to be our job. Squeekie was more likely to be rubbing against everyone who came in and lying on counters and tables to get people's attention. I preferred that no one talked with me or even looked at me, to be frank.

Especially now since I was freshly back from my spring haircut. I looked horrendous, and it was all Michelle's fault. It was also her fault that we had two new Castaway Critters, those freakishly friendly new cats who were put in the store—in my space—in an effort to get them adopted. Whatever, as long as they stayed away from me.

And yet no matter how many times I told them I wanted nothing to do with them, they still accosted me.

"Oh, Annika, you look fabulous, like a lioness! So smooth, so lovely!"

This new one was worse than all the others bundled together.

"Oh, I wish I had your fur, your fierceness," she continued without taking a breath.

And then, saints preserve me, she did the cat equivalent of a giggle.

I turned my back on her and walked away to find Squeekie. I had one more trick in my mane of normally beautiful hair—well, at least it was beautiful before I looked like someone had taken a weed whacker to me. I knew it would grow back but until it did, I was determined to be cranky. Or at least crankier than usual.

In any case, I had something that would make Squeekie drop his paintbrushes and stop preening in front of a crowd, so he'd come help me. And then maybe Michelle would stop screeching about not being able to find books that customers were asking for.

I finally found him on one of the walkways high above the customers. He liked to lounge up there. I was fine with that as long as it wasn't in the space I liked to occupy and wasn't during a time when I needed him working.

"All right, look, we have a problem." I booped him on the nose with my shorn paw to get his attention when he didn't look at me.

Finally, Squeekie turned his head toward me and cocked it sideways. Good, at least he was listening.

"The catnip is missing." Maybe if I could get him to look around I could gently but forcefully guide him to what I actually wanted him to do. Yes, it was sneaky, but that was my sparkling personality, and everyone could just deal with it. I'd tried direct and even a little bit nice and that hadn't gotten me anywhere, so now we moved to what I knew would work.

"Your ears look cute now that they're all cut. Do you need a brush to rub against? Michelle seems to like to use them along her palm. She brushes them back and forth and likes that."

I shook my head. He must have thought it was in answer to his question because he shrugged and looked below, probably searching out the next person he wanted to pet him. I, of course, had meant the head shake as an insult but kept that to myself. I needed him to help me find the books and catch those little menacing mice, who I knew were stealing them for some nefarious purposes. They were also taking pens and pencils, and that was driving Sam wild. So not only did I have to have my delicate ears assaulted by Michelle's displeasure, but I had to deal with Sam at the same time. It was too much for any cat, but me especially. They had no respect for the fact that I was already reluctant to be here, and this debacle was making it worse than usual.

Only by getting Squeekie to work with me would things settle down to the point where I could go back to my perch above the cash register without having to listen to everyone complain about the missing books and writing implements. Well, maybe not have Squeekie work with me so much as make him work.

"No, but did you not hear me? I just saw that the catnip is gone and so that means none for me and none at all for you." I let the statement hang there, hoping he'd get it so I wouldn't have to explain it to him. "I think those stupid mice took it."

Well, that got his attention. He ran down the walkway and vaulted to the floor. A customer yelped and threw her hands into the air as Squeekie began a hunt that ought to end up in several little fluffy things getting their tails handed to them. I chuckled in glee and stalked behind Squeekie just so I could have a front row seat.

We walked past the chalk outline of some dead person, over a crest from a school for kid wizards, then along the yellow brick road. Finally, we made it to a corner of the store in the romance section. Now he'd find them, and if they were indeed the culprits then they'd stop stealing books and I could very casually put back the catnip I'd hidden in the rafters above the hardbacks over by the bathroom

Michelle didn't like us going into. So what if we ended up in the toilet every once in a while? But she didn't like it and she was the owner, so everyone listened to her. Well, except me, but then I didn't have to. Which was why she'd posted a sign above the toilet to tell people to put the lid down.

But I was getting off topic, so I went back to watching Squeekie do what I'd asked him to do five days ago. He hunted for those furry little jerks and I sat on my rear end. The rear end that was far colder now on the concrete floor than before, since I had little to no fur on my behind due to the weed whacker. Just saying...

"Hey, guys, hey!" It was that irritating cat from the Castaway Critters, Dusty or Rusty or Musty or some other stupid name. Honestly, who named their cats that? But then it started talking. "Did I hear you were looking for the catnip? I just found it over near the bathroom. I didn't know the humans could get up there, even with that ladder. But I thought you might want a little bit from Michelle, so I brought it down. Maybe they'll let us have some now. As a treat."

Drat! Thwarted! And of course, now Squeekie and this menacing cat would take it to Michelle and Squeekie would lose all interest in doing my bidding.

"Thanks so much, Frida! We should definitely take it to Michelle. She's the sweetest and I know she'll be so happy to see us. She gets a little upset sometimes but she's always the nicest ever. I bet she's been missing it and wondered where it had gone. Good job!" Squeekie, well, squeaked.

Apparently, the cat's name had not been Musty or Dusty or Rusty, but Frida. It wasn't as regal as Annika, but it probably suited the cat. Not that I cared. And I would admit that Michelle didn't actually screech and was nice, but I would only admit that to myself. Certainly not to these two pansies.

Instead, I groaned and then groomed myself as they scampered away to the cash register where Michelle was apparently missing yet another book. Where were the little beasties hiding them? I tried to come up with a new idea on how to get Squeekie to look for them, but I had nothing. I was going to have to do this myself. I was not pleased by that prospect.

Rubbed the Wrong Way

So, while Squeekie and Frida trotted over to Michelle and Sam, I went on a prowl of my own. I stalked every corner, every hidden space and every square inch of our building. Well, not really. I went up to the rafters and sat up there contemplating how I could freefall on Squeekie without hurting myself or getting into trouble. But it did give me an oversight of the store and I started thinking about the other places they could hide books.

I was halfway to the loft where Michelle kept chairs when I was yet again accosted by this Frida cat.

"Hey, Annika! I saved you a piece of catnip. When you didn't come down with us, I figured you probably had something really important to do but I didn't want you to miss out, so I only took a small corner off and saved the rest for you. Enjoy!"

Could I push her over the side of the loft without getting in trouble? I looked down over the side and realized that Kristian, the painter of the floor murals and all-around too-nice person, was right below. So, she'd probably catch the castaway, and in the process, I'd get in trouble. Not worth it if there weren't going to be good results.

I just stared at Frida, who sat on her fluffy rear end and smiled at me. Fine, if it would get rid of her, I'd eat the catnip. After a few delicious bites, I stalked off again on my mission.

And she followed behind. How am I going to get rid of her?

It didn't matter though. I just kept going to each spot and being more and more irritated and disillusioned when I didn't find the many books that were missing.

After having covered everything above the store, I decided to go around the floor and check. It was almost closing time and at least I could avoid all those people cooing at me and trying to pet me. I only approached those I liked, and Michelle often said I could spot a bestseller as soon as the door opened, but other than that, I was not much for interaction.

I started at the register and strolled along the perimeter, going into the curtained-off room and around shelves, jumping on and off the table set up for people to talk books and do crafty-type things. Nothing appeared out of order, but I did see more empty slots on the shelves. Those mice were going to kill me with their thievery!

"What are we looking for? I already found the catnip. Do you need some more help? I like helping!"

"Look, Frito or whatever your name is, I don't need any help. Why don't you just go look all cute and stuff up front and hopefully someone will come in and take you far away?"

Frida just smiled at me. "No, that's okay. I like it here and helping is more fun than sitting in the cage."

I groaned. Seriously. I was never going to get away from this cat. Usually a few snippy words and they ran off to play with Squeekie or the toys in the cages, but not this one.

No more words were going to do any good, so I continued with my search. And found nothing. Drat again! Thwarted again!

I jumped up on the counter behind the new arrivals and licked myself again. At least not as much hair stuck on my tongue as usual. The haircut wasn't all bad, but I certainly wouldn't be thanking anyone for it.

"Watch out!" Frida yelled and then tackled me. I screeched and I clawed but got cut off when I heard a large crash on the floor and looked up to see a bunch of mice peeking over the edge of the air conditioning unit hanging in the rafters.

"Crap, we missed!" one of them squeaked and then they all giggled and rained down a plethora of pens and pencils and the rest of the things that had gone missing from the store. Those little jerks! They'd been trying to kill me by squashing me!

And Frida had, gulp, saved me. Well, crap was right. I was going to have to be nice and say thank you. Even I knew that.

So, I went and sniffed at Frida and even booped her on the nose. She smiled at me but didn't say anything else. It was possible we could be friendly, if not friends.

"Aw, look, Annika made a friend." Michelle came around the corner and then looked down to find all her missing books. "And you guys found them all! Extra treats for you! Good job!"

I took my treat and let Frida sit next to me as Michelle called all the customers to come get the books they'd wanted. The whole time Frida purred and even Squeekie came over at one point to sit with us.

And I'd bet catnip to irritating mice that Frida was going to be insufferable now that she'd kept me from getting squished. Instead of worrying about it, though, I'd just hope she'd get adopted and go away. To a good home, of course. But away. And soon.

Misty Simon

AUTHOR BIOGRAPHY

Misty Simon always wanted to be a storyteller…preferably behind a Muppet. Animal was number one, followed closely by Sherlock Hemlock… Since that dream didn't come true, she began writing stories to share her world with readers, one laugh at a time. She knows how to hula, was classically trained to sing opera, co-wrote her high school *Alma Mater,* and can't touch raw wood. Never hand her a Dixie cup with that wooden spoon/paddle thing. It's not pretty.

Touching people's hearts and funny bones are two of her favorite things, and she hopes everyone at least snickers in the right places when reading her books. She lives with her husband, daughter, and two insane dogs in Central Pennsylvania where she is hard at work on her next novel or three. She loves to hear from readers so drop her a line at misty@mistysimon.com.

7

Foofy McFluffster Saves the Day

Susan Dickinson

"Squeekie!" Annika called for her best friend as soon as the bookstore closed for the night. "Squeekie! You need to come here! Quickly!"

Squeekie lifted an eyelid at the same pace that Annika walks toward a human when her name is called. That is, *if* The Queen deigns to walk toward the human, at all. He was in less than a hurry to rush over to his best friend. After all, a beckoning Annika is nothing new. The last time she frantically called for him, she said it was urgent for him to hurry over to help her in the Science Fiction section. Little did he realize she was hiding in the Mystery section. 'YANK!' Pulling his tail as he passed; she galloped away, giggling hysterically and fully delighted with herself!

Squeekie loves spending the days with humans, but it's also nice and peaceful when it's dark outside. The whir of the fans running and cars driving by can really lull a tired kitty to sleep. Squeekie was napping on his favorite book. Some books are just more comfortable than others.

"Unless you just found a giant bag full of treats, I'm not budging." Squeekie rolled upside-down a bit more.

"Ugh," she muttered. Annoyed, Annika grabbed a small square of fabric with her teeth, jerked it into the air, and brought it over to Squeekie. She dropped it on his hind legs. "Look at all the colorful capes Michelle left at the store, tonight."

"So?" Squeekie wisecracked; failing miserably as he tried kicking it off his legs. "How do you know what they are? They look like rags to me. Maybe there is an arts and crafts event next week, or maybe she will use them to wipe the counters." 'KICK, JERK, JOLT!' Squeekie finally shook the rest of the cloth off his foot after spending a full minute trying to free his leg from the silly rag.

"These are capes!" Annika proclaimed. "These capes will turn us into the superheroes I know we are! Well, at least for me. I'm not sure you're qualified to be a superhero." With that, Annika picked up the cloth and turned to leave, but Squeekie stomped his paw down on its edge.

"Heyyyy, what do you mean by that?"

"Everyone thinks you're the good-natured one and I'm the difficult one, but you and I know the truth," Annika declared.

Squeekie looked at her in disbelief. "Annika, that *is* the truth. Anyone who has ever visited the store knows that!"

Annika twitched her tail right across Squeekie's nose as she sauntered away with her prized cape still in her teeth. "Everyone will know the truth when I become a superhero and you can't be as super as I am." She quickly whirled around, throwing the cape across her back. The glint in her eye and smirk on her face became more impish and defiant than usual. "I am Foofy McFluffster, the crime-fighting cloud." She sauntered up the ramp by the Read Harder books near the register. She shouted down: "I float from place to place, taking the bad guys by surprise and disappearing into thin air to escape their clutches." At that moment, Annika instantly started hovering in mid-air above the catwalk! She floated over to the Historical Fiction shelves. Was she using her dark magic, again?

"I can listen to all their evil plots, all their despicable schemes, and all the celebrations they have when they do bad things and brag about it. I can tell all this to the authorities so the bad guys get nabbed. Foofy McFluffster saves the day! Foofy McFluffster gets all the treats!" She quickly floated down into the Mystery aisle and came sauntering out from behind the bookcase.

"How did you do that?" Squeekie could not believe what he just saw.

"It's my *cape*. I *told* you! It's the last piece I needed to complete the superhero puzzle in my life. I guess you're not excited about the capes since you don't think you have superpowers like I do. You can't transform from a common bookstore cat into a magical, beautiful, soft cloud of fluff. Can you?"

Squeekie went from being in awe of Annika's super powers to being irritated. Annika can be difficult; it's part of her charm as the Reluctant Bookstore Cat. On the other hand, she's not usually *quite* this insulting.

Squeekie shook his head. How did she know she had superpowers? Why did she call him a "common bookstore cat?"

Chewie, an adoptable bookstore cat, came wandering over from his nap. "Hi guys. What are you doing? Can I play, too?"

Annika rebuffed "Hey, kid. You want to be part of our crime-fighting team? Do you have any superpowers?"

"Um...I don't think so." Chewie, looked at Squeekie for confirmation.

"Don't worry, kid. Squeekie doesn't have them, either," Annika bragged, "so you can hang out with him while Foofy is fighting crime and winning everyone's admiration and treats."

"Who?"

Squeekie broke in: "The only difference between you and me, Annika, is that you already knew about your powers, and that you just needed a cape! I'll bet if I put on a cape, I would have the same powers as you. Maybe mine will be even better!"

"Oh, *now* you're excited about your cape. I told you! Go pick one out and try it on." Annika dared. She showed Squeekie the pile of Michelle's fabric squares and he started looking through. Too red, too stripey, too scratchy, to slippery, too thin, too ugly, not enough blue... Blue! "I got it!" Squeekie tossed the cape over his shoulder and paraded around the floor. He trotted back over to Chewie. "How do I look?"

Chewie said, "I don't care what Annika says, I think you look like you could save the day."

"I can be a superhero, too. See, Annika? You don't know what you're talking about."

"But can you fly?" she purred.

Squeekie tried hard. He tried harder than when he tried to stop Annika from swiping the new kitten's treats. He closed his eyes, whirled his tail, and jumped! Nothing. He looked over at Chewie, who looked back at him with a glint of hope and belief behind those white whiskers. There's *no way* Annika could be right. Then again...

"I know what to do!" Squeekie ran over to the ramp and headed up to the catwalk. He walked above the adoptable cat cages and looked down to the floor. "The magic happens when you need it most. That's the whole point behind being a superhero." Squeekie sucked in his soft belly, puffed out his chest, and counted out loud: One meow. Two meows. Three!

On three, Squeekie jumped! Superhero magic is sure to hold us in its embrace like a human hug and whisk us off our paws to...

'SPLAT!!!!'

Squeekie landed almost – but not quite – on all four paws. His blue cape wrapped itself across his eyes and he stumbled. Stunned, he shook his head, splayed out his paws, and sat there, utterly dumbfounded. Chewie stared while Annika fell over in fits of laughter. She dragged herself across the yellow brick road and into the Mystery aisle. Within a few seconds, she was floating in the air, again.

"So, Squeekie. Your superhero name is "Rocky." You sink like a rock! But don't worry; you must have some type of talent to offer. Detective McFluffster is on the case." And with that, Annika floated down to the ground where Squeekie was sitting. She hopped to the side and revealed what was underneath all her magnificent floof: one of those big, metallic bugs that the humans go nuts over! One of the visiting authors must have left it here by accident. The books in the Science section of the back room call them "drones."

Squeekie heard a tiny, muffled giggle from the corner of the Civil War collection. He and Chewy twisted their heads around and saw one of the newest adoptable kittens, holding the direction-a-ma-bobber-thingy that made Annika's metal bug fly. Kids these days and their technology!

Squeekie looked at Chewy. "*This* is why I make every effort to get to the new kids when they arrive. It is *critical* that I reach them before Annika does."

Foofy McFluffster Saves the Day

    Squeekie threw a low growl in Annika's general direction. "Just wait until you have a *real* emergency someday." But Annika didn't hear him over all her tears and laughter. Good thing she was wearing that cape so she could dry her eyes before her beautiful coat got wet. Foofy McFluffster has a reputation to uphold!

Susan Dickinson

AUTHOR BIOGRAPHY

Susan Dickinson has been a huge fan of felines since birth. She has taken care of cats her entire life and more recently volunteered at the Humane Society for 10 years as a cat socializer. Some have called her a "cat whisperer" to explain the most ornery cats' affinity for her.

She has been a huge fan of Annika's for years, ever since Annika walked up to Susan and demanded to be petted. Susan eventually left the bookstore - unscathed - realizing a friendship had begun.

Susan loves travelling the world and spends her time appreciating and participating in sports, the fine arts, new and fun food & beverages, business writing, and studying leadership, (occupational hazards resulting from her business degrees from Bloomsburg University and Penn State University). Originally from Wayne County, PA, she currently works in Harrisburg and lives in Mechanicsburg with her co-author and best friend, Gobbler. Gobbler's floof and sassy disposition were important contributions to the creative process.

The name "Foofy McFluffster" came to Susan in a dream weeks before the Annika book was announced, so she was delighted to find this way to share the adorable name with everyone.

8

The Princess Tower

Donna L. Leiss

"It's go time," Annika announced in her Eartha Kitt Catwoman-esque voice sending her plan into motion.

She got to work turning off the store's alarm and unlocking the door with her claws. Meanwhile, the foster cats pushed books off the shelves onto the top of their rolling crates, which were quickly headed out the opened door. Annika followed, car keys dangling from her mouth. The mice took to their forced task of distracting Squeekie by scattering in all directions with tiny satchels of catnip attached to their backs. Annika had earlier made a persuasive case for them to help; "Do it or be dinner."

Annika led the gang to *her* electric Fiat- the white one picturing half her flat Himalayan face with ANNIKA THE RELUCTANT BOOKSTORE CAT on the door below the name of her home, CUPBOARD MAKER BOOKS. The foster cats stopped rolling their temporary homes on a dime and the books atop flew through the car's half-open window and onto the driver's seat. Annika assumed her position upon them and inserted the key into the ignition as the others snatched blankets from the crates and joined her inside the running car.

The radio came to life and Cyndi Lauper sang out "Girls Just Wanna Have Fun", while Henry, tapped the nearest pet store's address into the GPS. That set, Annika jabbed the D button on the electronic transmission shifter pad with her pinky toe.

"Punch it, kitty," Annika commanded to the Calico named Cecil, tasked with working the accelerator.

The car flew forward pinning Henry and his mates, the sister and brother duo Fred and Ginger, to the passenger seat while Annika clung to the steering wheel for dear life with all four paws.

"Brake! Brake!" Annika cried. Joe, a silver tabby, jumped on the brake just before the car careened onto the highway. Annika's face hit the steering wheel. Henry, Fred, and Ginger became one ball of fur as they rolled forward from the jolt.

"Gently, guys!" Annika hissed to Joe and Cecil. Her perpetual sourpuss face sourer.

After some deep breaths, Annika instructed Cecil to slowly press the gas pedal. She steered the car left as the GPS instructed, straightening it out between the lines just in time to inform Joe to slow down for another left. After a sharp right followed by a quick sharp left, Fred, who was turning green, clamped his mouth with his paw.

"DO NOT throw up in this car! Hang your head out the window," Annika shrieked at Fred.

But as Annika focused back on the road, her frown turned slightly upwards. She was enjoying herself. She reveled in the night air blowing on her face as the car twisted and turned. The air of freedom suited her much better than the air blower the groomer used on her after her forced "haircut" that made her look like a tiny lion. Didn't her human captors understand she couldn't be tamed? She wasn't dubbed the "Reluctant Bookstore Cat" for nothing. And they should give in to her every demand like the princess she was? Which is why she took it upon herself to get the princess tower Mother Michelle had shown her a picture of, but denied her the real thing.

Annika, so entrenched in her thoughts, missed the electronic voice informing her they had arrived at their destination.

"Annika! We're here!" Henry said. There was no reaction from Annika, so he used a claw to get her attention.

"What the...?" Annika started, glaring in his direction.

"We're here!" Henry yelled.

At this, Annika turned the wheel hard, foregoing her instruction to Joe to brake. The Fiat took flight up over the curb of the landscaped parking lot island and drifted across the pet store parking lot like the hot rods in *The Fast and the Furious*. The car was awhirl with wide-eyed bouncing cats.

"Brake!" Annika yelled.

Joe jumped hard on the brake leaving a trail of burnt rubber as the car spun before coming to a hard hockey stop in the front row parking spot. Breathing hard, Annika slowly unhooked her pinky claw from the steering wheel to put the car in park.

"Oh gosh, where's Fred?" Ginger asked looking towards the back seat. "Fred?!"

"I'm okay," Fred called from outside the car. "I jumped out while we were spinning. I couldn't hold it in any longer," he explained with a belch, wiping his mouth with his paw.

Annika took the girly-pink bandana they forced upon her after her humiliating "hair cut" and tied it around her head like a babushka, as Henry and Ginger dragged Michelle's jacket from the back seat.

"Are we ready, guys?" Annika asked. They all responded in the affirmative, even Cecil, who stayed behind in case they needed a fast getaway. "Remember," she added, "tails tucked."

Annika, atop the other cats, hissed out directions to her feet (Joe's feet) to the cat section. They rocked like a drunken sailor, but the bored teenager behind the counter paid them no mind. The humongous cat tower at the back of the store loomed larger and larger as they neared it. Annika, gob-smacked by its wondrous glory, forgot to instruct Joe to stop and they all ran straight into the tower's base, threatening to topple them. The tower gave the slightest wiggle.

"Isn't it awesome?" said a voice from behind them, causing them to collectively jump in fear and then settle back down into one. The pet store worker didn't seem to notice as he continued, "It would be great for all the cats at your bookstore, Michelle."

Annika stiffened until she remembered the Cupboard Maker Books jacket with Michelle's name embroidered on the front of it.

"Should I put one on your account and load it in your car?" the man said, whose name was Phil, according to the name tag on his vest.

A satisfying grin emerged on Annika's face as she nodded her head.

"I'll get one from the back," Phil said.

Before he started down the aisle, Annika handed him a large, luxurious maroon velvet pillow with golden tassels and a container full of catnip filled toys to add to the order.

They followed Phil out of the store who asked, "Did you do something different with your hair, Michelle? You look different."

The human women were right, Annika thought, *men are clueless.* She nodded to Phil as he maneuvered the large box into the hatchback.

Closing the back, Phil said, "Okay, you're all set."

Annika nodded in response. Phil stood there staring at her, which made her nervous. It was awkward. Annika reached into the jacket pocket and found human currency. She reached her hand to Phil's opened palm and accidently scratched him with her claw.

"Ouch," Phil uttered as he dropped the cash. "Get your nails done too, Michelle?" Phil asked as he bent down to retrieve the money just as the store closed and the parking lot lights dimmed.

By the time he stood up, the cats were back in the car and Annika had instructed the waiting Cecil to, once again, "Punch it, kitty!"

The car swerved wildly through the parking lot as Annika attempted to watch the road and Phil's reaction in the rearview mirror. She relaxed when he turned and walked back into the store.

The cats in the passenger seat were giving each other high-fives. Henry imitated Phil, "*Did you do something different with your hair, Michelle?*" making himself, Fred, and Ginger roll with laughter. Annika began to join in the laughter, until she spotted flashing red and blue flashing lights behind them. She tensed and hissed out a command to the others. The car slowed and Annika directed it to the side of the road. She again donned the pink bandana and wrapped herself in a blanket from one of the cat's crates. She lowered the window as the police officer approached with his flashlight.

The Princess Tower

"License and registration, please ...um... Ma'am?" the officer requested as he shone the light in Annika's blue eyes making her squint. "We got a call of a vehicle driving erratically and there's part of a bush stuck to the bumper of your car," he stated.

She pointed to graphics the driver's side door displaying her face and name below the name of the bookstore. She then pointed to her collar and tags.

"Oh, yes, Cupboard Maker Books. This is Michelle's car," the officer said as he shone the flashlight around the car. He did a double take on the passenger seat. Henry, Fred, and Ginger arranged a flattened cardboard cutout of Michelle, used at the launch of her fabulous debut novel, in the seat. Only Michelle's face was visible, while her jacket served as the torso and a blanket covered the legs.

"Oh, Michelle. There you are. Is everything okay?" the officer asked the corrugated imposter. The cats in the jacket raised one arm to the cardboard forehead and the other to the mouth. Annika delicately pushed the flashlight off of the cardboard face. She put her paw to her lips to shush the officer.

"Oh. You have a migraine and you're sick," the officer guessed. To bolster this theory, Ginger faked a hairball. The officer grimaced. Annika pointed up the road towards the bookstore. "Okay," the officer said, "I'm going to let you off with a Warning, but please take it easy. Hope you feel better, Michelle," to which the fake Michelle saluted. The officer handed Annika the paper warning and removed the leaves and twigs from the bumper as he walked back to his cruiser. No one made a sound or a move until they pulled into the bookstore parking lot.

After they rolled in the purchases on the previously abandoned foster cats' crates, Annika relocked the door and rearmed the security system. She threw Squeekie a new catnip stuffed toy before she sliced open the cat tower box with her claws. The excitement on Annika's face, all of their faces, curdled when they realized the tower wasn't in one magnificent piece like in the store, but in three separate pieces to fit into the box. It was going to be a long night putting the tower together, especially with not having opposable thumbs. Thankfully, the assembly instructions included pictures.

The evening was filled with fun and free reign of the treat jar. Annika even joined in the merriment, foregoing her typical grumpiness. Everyone helped put the tower together, including Squeekie and the mice. It was dawn when they finished setting it up in the back, left corner of the store, and one by one, all with stuffed bellies, they took to their sleeping areas with a "Good night". With her new, velvet pillow in mouth, Annika leapt up her princess tower to her rightful place on top.

As she climbed, the tower gave a shimmy, but she thought nothing of it and happily hunkered down on her pillow. She overlooked everything, and from this vantage point, she saw the bookstore in a whole new light. It wasn't her initial idea of a home, with its rows of seemingly endless books, customers in and out, and the occasional annoyance of a young foster cat wanting to play, but it was her home. She adored her best friend Squeekie, although she'll never admit to it, and all the attention she received. In that moment, Annika became content with being a bookstore cat and she sunk into a deep sleep.

Annika was so exhausted she never heard the commotion outside, nor the bell ring on the door when Mother and Sam came into open the store. However, she heard Mother slam the books on the counter; the ones left in the driver's seat of the car. It scared Annika so, she jumped with fright, forgetting she was on top of her very tall princess tower. Annika banged her head on the ceiling and plummeted back down upon her pillow so fast it made the tower start to wobble. The earlier shimmy was not an anomaly, but a clue the tower was not put together correctly.

"What the heck? I cannot believe this!" Michelle shouted.

"Um, Michelle," Sam said noticing the tall tower swaying in the back of the store.

But Michelle was on a rant and continued, "Someone took these books, took the car, scratched the left bumper, got stopped by the cops, and made fraudulent purchases with my credit card!"

"Michelle!" Sam exclaimed and turned Michelle around.

The Princess Tower

They both witnessed the tall tower sway too far to the right, causing it to knock into the closest book shelf, which sent it cascading into the next, and the next, and the next. Books upon books slammed to the ground, while Annika skittered across the top of the shelves like a first time ice skater without balance. Michelle and Sam ran towards the action arriving only when the last shelf hit the wall and Annika was tossed into Michelle's arms like a baby.

Annika quivered and clung to Michelle like she never had before, but that did not deflect the wraith that came afterward. After seeing the cat tower in the store, Michelle had no doubt it was Annika behind everything. Michelle seethed while the store was closed to upright all the shelves and restock the books. She threatened to ship Annika off to another home, but in the end Michelle forgave Annika who became "the not-so-much-anymore reluctant bookstore cat". Michelle even kept the princess cat tower in the store (correctly assembled), but Annika didn't need it. She realized she was in a loving home with family who already treat her like a princess.

Donna L. Leiss

AUTHOR BIOGRAPHY

Donna Leiss has been in love with reading, writing, art, and music since she was a little girl. She is the author of two published short stories: "The Black Dress" in the anthology Strange Magic, and "The Nine Lives of Squeekie" published in the collection The Second and Third Nine Lives of Squeekie the Bookstore Cat. She is an alumnus of Elizabethtown College, a member of Penn Writers, and has completed novel writing courses given by the Perry County Council of the Arts. Donna currently resides in Middletown, PA with her husband and two Siberian huskies where she continues to create.

Connect with Donna on her Facebook page at https://www.facebook.com/dllwrites and on Twitter @dllwrites.

*The Very, Very Bad Misadventures of
Annika the Reluctant Bookstore Cat*

Note on Stories 8 - 12

Stories 8 through 12 were written by the owner and employees of the Cupboard Maker Books. They were not included in the judging as they were the judges.

Annika the Reluctant Bookstore Cat

9

The Story of My Mysterious Past
Michelle Haring

All of my fans ask my history and I don't want to answer because I want them to see me as an international cat of mystery. I'd rather be mysterious than tragic.

I was born to Himalayan parents and I had siblings, but as an eight week old kitten, Miss Betty bought me to be her companion. On my first day at her home, she dragged me from my comfortable cat carrier and stood over the short metal fence in her yard with me clutched in her hands.

She showed me to her next door neighbor, Michelle. I remember her words these seven years later because they burned into my skull. "You always told me that you wanted a Himalayan cat. I won't outlive her. Will you take her when I'm gone?"

Michelle replied, "Betty, you could outlive her, but I promise that I will care for her when you're gone."

Miss Betty had just bought me. She upended my entire life but she was supposed to be my forever person. I wanted to be the center of her life and her companion.

Miss Betty waved my tiny body at Michelle. She smacked her lips and shook her head. "I'm seventy eight years old. I'll die before this little cat, and I want to be sure that she's safe."

Michelle nodded her head, but there was a sad glint in her eye. "I promise, but I hope that you live a long time with her."

Five years passed with Miss Betty as my sole companion. No one visited her. She told me that she didn't have any nearby family or friends that lived close to her. Sometimes, I wanted to explore and I'd sneak out of the house. Miss Betty yelled at me and threatened to send me over to Michelle's early. I knew she wouldn't do it, because she was my best friend.

Every day Miss Betty fed me and petted me, but then one day she couldn't get out of bed. She cried and I cried. My fear won out over my hunger. Something was wrong with my best friend and I couldn't purr or nudge her to make her feel better. For three days, we huddled on her bed. I didn't know what would become of us. I worried about her and I fretted about my stomach. If Miss Betty didn't get up, I didn't know if I would ever eat again.

Then I heard the pounding on the door. "Open up! This is the police, we are doing a welfare check." I ran to the door, but without opposable thumbs, opening it was beyond my abilities. I cried for help because I knew that Miss Betty couldn't but my cries were so quiet. I don't think anyone heard me.

If Squeekie were there, they would have heard him. Everyone can hear Squeekie when he cries.

The pounding on the door got louder and the police broke Miss Betty's door open. In my terror, I almost ran out the front door, but Miss Betty needed me so I followed the policeman to her room.

She yelled, "Where's my cat? Where's my Annika? Did she escape when you broke my door? If you lost my cat, I'll have your job."

My lady was a feisty one and she loved me so much. I jumped on her bed and when she saw me, she reached toward me but she couldn't move or grab me like she usually did. I tried to go to her but the police officer said, "Ma'am we're going to need to take you to the hospital. I'm sorry but your cat can't come with you. Is there anyone who can take care of her?"

Miss Betty croaked out the command, "Go to The Cupboard Maker Books. My neighbor Michelle owns it and she promised to take Annika if I couldn't take care of her."

I dashed from the room. I didn't want to live with the neighbor. I saw all of her cats in the windows of her house. They looked mean and there were so many of them. One was gigantic with long hair like mine but all colors of brown and black, another one looked like me with buff colored fur and a long puffy tail, a different one was white with a little orange on the tips of it's ears, and the scariest one of all looked like a nasty short haired alley cat with orange and white fur.

I was supposed to be an only cat with my only person. I wasn't meant to live with other cats and so many people. I saw Michelle, a man and a boy in that house. Nope, nope, nope, I counted on my life being me and Miss Betty.

I hid under the bed and cried when the people carried my lady out of the house. She only left me for short amounts of time every week. She always came back smelling funny with her hair in tight curls. The food for her showed up every day from people that knocked on the door and called it meals on wheels. For the last year, Betty wasn't hungry and the food rotted on the counters. She fed me special cat food but shooed me away from her meals on the counters.

I felt terror that everyone would forget about me with Betty in the hospital. I also feared going to the house next door with all of the meanies. As I quivered under the bed, the door opened and a lady came into the room with a cage in her hands. She peered under the bed and grabbed me. I hadn't been put in a cage since I was a kitten. I hated it.

The next thing I knew, she put me in a car and drove me away from house. I thought they were sending me next door. A car shouldn't have been part of this transaction. I thought Michelle must have lied to Betty, and they were planning to take me to the place where unwanted kitties go.

Instead, the lady who caged me took me and the cage into a gigantic block building with beautiful pictures painted on the outside. She opened the door and said, "Hi, I'm from Animal Control, and I'm bringing you Annika."

I recognized Michelle as she peered into my cage. She cooed at me, "Annika, I'm so sorry about Betty. I know your whole life will be different. You are going to be a bookstore cat and live here."

A bookstore cat that sounded even worse than living with all of those cats at Michelle's house. I didn't even know what a bookstore was. Then they put the cage on the floor, and I met Squeekie for the first time.

Michelle Haring

I hissed, but he yawned at me to show me his huge fangs. I have pretty, tiny teeth, not scary ones that could puncture my arteries even with all of my fur to protect me. I couldn't help but notice his gorgeous blue eyes, shiny beige coat and elegant bow tie. I found myself drawn to him in spite of my fear.

Michelle introduced me to him, "Squeekie, this is Annika. She will live here with your forever. This is her forever home. You won't ever be lonely again."

I cried, because I knew I'd never be able to go home again. I refused to speak to this cat or his human who promised me to him like I was an object. I was so afraid that I froze when they moved me to a bigger metal cage. That entire day, I shook and wailed. The human kept coming back and trying to comfort me while Squeekie stood outside the came and purred at me.

This place smelled like other cats and there were kittens galloping around the store. They were all free and I was trapped. It was terrible during the day when the people kept coming and trying to touch me. Then night arrived. The people turned the lights off and said, "Squeekie, take care of Annika for us."

Squeekie listened to them and stayed next to the cage all night long. He told me his story of living with the wonderful, red haired lady in his time before the bookstore. He shared stories about all of the cats that passed through his bookstore on the way to their forever homes. Many of the cat tales revolved around Mac and Matilda. They lived with Squeekie for two years and disappeared within a month of each other. Squeekie fell asleep in the middle of a sentence.

I never told him how much he helped me on my first night. That night Squeekie became my best friend.

The Story of My Mysterious Past

AUTHOR BIOGRAPHY

Michelle Haring is the co-owner of Cupboard Maker Books. She loves all cats but especially Annika and Squeekie. She reads approximately a book a day but writes much slower than that.

Annika the Reluctant Bookstore Cat

10

I'm the Center of My World

Kristian Beverly

I cannot believe the humans. They've *really* done it this time. I press my nose against the walls of the cage. Maybe if I head butt it, it'll open enough so I can escape. Or if the metal parts clink together, the humans will tire of keeping me captive and will release me. Either way, I want my paws touching the floor and no pattern of squares in front of my eyes.

I press once more against the cage and a gap opens. I slip out and land on the floor. My tail whips back and forth in annoyance. Behind me, Squeekie is still sleeping. How can he just continue sleeping like that? Plus, it's his fault that we were put into the cage in the first place. The humans reasoned that because the doors would be open, for our safety we had to be put into a secure location. I would never walk out of the door, but again, Squeekie is more kitten brain than cat when presented with new experiences.

Squeekie opens his eyes. *Annika, how are you out there? The humans said we had to stay in here.*

I tilt my head. *Clearly I didn't want to do that. Plus the rule's for you since you always try to eat the grass at the door.*

Squeekie sits up and looks guiltily down at his paws. But it's true! No matter how many times he gets sprayed with water, he still tries to thrust his head out of the door to snag a piece of grass. Kitten brain—that's all Squeekie's head is filled of. He doesn't think past a minute ahead.

I trot out of the food area and start walking past cases of books. The concrete's cool on my paws the closer I step to the door. I let my tail hang loose between my legs so the humans don't think I've forgiven them for sticking me in the cage. It smells like plants out here. Every week, boxes of food are brought in and the humans squeal at the items instead of the box. They claim that Squeekie and I can't control ourselves with the door wide open. That's merely one of us—and he's the one that can't figure out how to get out.

But the outside does fascinates me. Never enough to do what Squeekie does nor actually step outside though. I step up to the door and stare out of it.

The sky's dark and moody, no wispy clouds. Instead the clouds look heavy and dark. But it still makes for interesting watching.

"Annika!" a two legged feeder says. "You know you shouldn't be there."

I actually shouldn't be out of the cage, but I can't actually say this. Since the humans can't understand my words, I have trained them to understand my eyes. It's still a work in progress.

The two legged feeder wouldn't dare spray me with their water. No, humans. It took long enough to break the habit, but when I'm annoyed I slip into kitten brain. I eventually got it across to them that I am not stupid, I clearly know this is my home and the outside is full of sticky weather, wet ground, and more people than I'd know what to do with. Still, sometimes they worry when I stare out of the door that I'll walk out. It's hard enough to keep my toes clean in here. Imagine all of the dirt and icky slimy that'd need dealt. No thank you.

I turn my head and stare at the *human*. They say my glare is legendary. She pokes out her lips like a kitten. Such things do not work on me so I turn my head back to glance outside.

I am Annika. My first human mother said she'd named me after a goddess. And goddesses are powerful and beautiful. I don't back down. My fur puffs up and my tail flips back and forth.

Bright lights hit the door and I step back. No use asserting my claim to royalty right now. Humans park their car and amble through the parking lot before one wraps their hand around the door handle. The door pops open, and the outdoor sounds amplify before being sucked out again. Humans resemble kittens. They always

I'm the Center of My World

want to use their fingers to touch-touch-touch. Why must everything be felt? Why can't it be viewed or even smelled?

"Oh what a pretty kitty!" the first human says. She wears a frilly dress and her hair falls down her back. I wouldn't like my fur to be that long.

I realize now that the people who walk through the door are not here for me. I am a side show attraction. When this place first became my home I'd suspected that I had inherited a kingdom full of beds, and cat highways. While I imagined being a queen here required some interactions with humans, I didn't imagine that it revolved around their ignoring me. But at least I eventually realized this. Squeekie is a few years older than me and he still doesn't get it. He still falls under kitten brain in having the whole world revolve around him. As if he's a star and that's why everyone bounds over to him. But if he's the star, I'm the queen of this world.

I am embarrassed to even say this, but the few times I craved human attention I actually used my voice. Humans are silly in how they stare at pieces of books. . Their mouths sometime droop in sadness or curve up in happiness. I don't understand the need to stare at things that give such different responses. I give the same response. *Don't touch me, admire.*

When I want to perform, I flip up my tail. My forepaw gets lifted and arch my back. If you have a camera—I'll perform even better. I will sit and cock my head, blinking my big eyes. The humans say they are blue, but humans use all sorts of words to describe things that can be summed up much simpler. The best word to describe me is beautiful. Or queen. Either of those I'll answer to. I've noticed that humans enjoy two things (other than books): fluffy cats and kittens. And kittens don't understand the importance of human attention. But I do.

I dash away from the newest humans, and trot past the counter. The bookstore human leans over and smacks her lips. She wants my attention, which I'll reward her with since she did not spray me. She smiles and I continue forward. Books contain so many different smells. They tell stories of long ago trips, of other creatures that have brushed against their pages. Humans see the contents—but I taste home.

Kristian Beverly

I'm not one hundred percent sure when I realized I was not the center of the world. A tragic realization I must say. Even as a newborn kitten, where the world was yet a vivid collection of sounds and shapes, my mother made me feel like the center of the universe. Her nose pressed against me, and I snuggled into her long, warm fur. Reflecting back, she gave us all the same amount of love but I convinced myself that I earned more. The hot, smooth hands of humans constantly touched and prodded at me. As my hearing developed I adopted the views of the humans. They said things like *well she's going to be a beauty* or *this is the best one of the litter*. Such phrases, even before understanding the gravity of what they mean, really singe their way into your head. When the beginning of your life is surrounded by you being the best, of course you develop the sense that you truly are *the* gift to the universe.

As the newest group of humans herd towards the door, their arms are full of books. I press myself to the wall and watch them. They glance at me and there are a few smiles. Once upon a time ago I believed I was the center of the universe. Now? I'm good with being the center of this smaller one.

I'm the Center of My World

AUTHOR BIOGRAPHY

Kristian Beverly loves to write and has been writing her whole life. Before being able to write, she just illustrated her stories but now she writes short fiction and novels. When not writing, Kristian can be found on the back of a horse, creating art, or reading.

Annika the Reluctant Bookstore Cat

11

Queen Annika of the Goblins

Samantha Coons

Somebody, or something, was picking on Squeekie. And Annika didn't like it.

And things that Annika didn't like were *taken care of.*

The whole business began on one of those days when the humans stayed in her bookstore longer than they were welcome. Those days came about once or twice every seven days, but just because they weren't constant didn't mean she would tolerate them.

Humans were lucky they were so much bigger than she was. *So* lucky.

In any case, that day when the humans stayed past her welcome, Squeekie started acting…strange.

He brought out a paintbrush to show off to the humans. This was not strange, or not strange for Squeekie at least.

But when Human Boss leaned over to pet him, he had his back turned to her, and when her hand touched his fur he, well he…

Flinched.

Squeekie never flinched away from anyone, not in the whole two years she'd known him. Cats who flinched had *stories*. Stories about the kind of humans that Annika would *take care of* once she figured out a foolproof plan to take over the world.

Squeekie had no stories like that. He had many stories of human children dragging him around the store, and many more of human adults dragging him around the store. But they all meant well, and told him how pretty he was, so he didn't mind.

But now he flinched, and Annika would find the one responsible and make them regret the day they messed with her best friend.

Annika tiptoed through the dark store, her dainty feet making no sound against the wooden floor. Squeekie retreated at the smallest noise lately, and she didn't want him running off before she found out what she needed to know.

She headed straight for the small cat tower near the window, where Squeekie holed up the last few weeks after lights out. This particular cat tower was really more of a stool than a proper tower, with two holes built into the side.

Squeekie hid in the lower hole, curled up tight and staring out at the bookstore.

Annika meowed softly as she approached, and she made sure he saw her as she rounded the corner. She slowly padded over to him when he squeaked back to her, and she sniffed over his face.

"You're hiding," she said, "and I don't like it."

Squeekie mewed and hid his face. She narrowed her eyes.

"That's not an answer."

Paws skittered above them on the wooden catwalks. Squeekie flinched farther into the cat tree while Annika directed her displeasure upwards.

The current foster kittens chased each other, yelling across the store as they scampered harum-scarum above the bookshelves.

She would have to bat them on the head a few times later.

She faced Squeekie again and drew herself up, poofing her fur out.

"Tell me why you keep flinching, or I won't help you get extra treats anymore."

"But that's not fair," Squeekie yowled.

She swatted him on the ear to make her point clear. He yowled again but she stayed poofy.

"Fine," he said, rubbing his ear with a paw, "A couple of days ago I went down into the basement, and I found another set of stairs. And I went down those, because I thought maybe there would be something interesting at the bottom."

Annika would normally roll her eyes, but she didn't want to risk interrupting him. *She* knew it was best to send someone else first when exploring, but Squeekie could be a little slow, or as the humans called it - kind.

"But when I reached the bottom there were these horrible goblin things who kept pinching me and calling me names, and they wouldn't let me leave for a long, long time. Eventually I slipped past them and the basement friends promised me they'd guard the stairway to make sure the goblin things wouldn't follow. But they were awful, and I'm afraid they'll come back."

The tip of Annika's tail flicked back and forth.

"I see," she said.

She flipped herself around toward the back of the store. Squeekie jumped out and snagged a hunk of the fur on her behind.

She hissed and pulled herself out of his grasp.

"Don't go there," he yowled, "you might get hurt, and then I'll be sad."

His eyes watered and his ears lay flat on his head. He looked quite pitiful, and for a moment Annika almost felt bad.

Almost.

"Nothing is scarier than me," she sniffed and pranced away from Squeekie. He yowled but didn't follow, to her relief. The rescue kittens above paid her no mind, because they were just smart enough to know not to bother her.

She hurried through the store as fast as she could while maintaining her dignity, which wasn't difficult as her every movement radiated dignity.

She slowed down once she reached the normal basement steps. Annika did not often go into the basement. She didn't really like the 'basement friends,' as Squeekie called them. She found them a little too unsettling.

Also it was difficult to go down the stairs in a dignified manner. She managed, of course, but an outsider observer might mistake it for scampering down, or even scurrying down. But no, she was Annika, and Annika did not scurry like a mouse or scamper like a puppy. Her *every* movement was dignified.

After not scurrying, nor scampering, she stood at the foot of the basement steps and peered into the dark cavern.

She regretted not asking Squeekie for more details about where to find his mysterious second set of stairs, but it would have taken ten times as long if she had stopped to ask for details. No, she was correct to keep the conversation brief, as she was always correct in everything.

She circled a few times near the staircase, making sure the second stair weren't nestled into the wall there. Meanwhile, the basement friends sat against the opposite walls, watching her but making no move beyond the occasional wriggle. She shuddered and hoped Squeekie's stairs weren't anywhere near them.

She poked her nose under the stairway and around a few piles of boxes. Musty and cold. Nothing out of the ordinary for the basement. She hopped up onto the box pile to check the old window, but the only view was dirt, same as always.

Then movement flashed in the corner of her eye, and not the languid undulating of the basement friends. She spun around, fur fluffed up, and zeroed in on a hole in the wall that hadn't been there a moment before.

A small strange creature with a long skinny tail stood frozen, eyes wide as Annika focused her glare on it. It looked almost like a mouse, but it only had a few spots of scraggly fur and its toes were longer.

"You!" she screeched at it.

It stood still for a heartbeat before disappearing into the wall. Annika scrambled after it, intent on her prey and now longer worrying about dignity. She had bigger fish to fry. Or mice to fry. Whatever.

She slid into the hole in a second, sprinting down the rough stone stairs behind it. These stairs went on for much longer than the regular basement steps, but she didn't slow. Her playtime with Squeekie kept her in tip-top shape. She froze at the bottom with paws spread wide, ready for anything.

The thing waited for her, two identical creatures standing on either side of it with tiny horns poking out of the fur on their heads.

All three grinned at her with pointed teeth, eyebrows drawn down in a leer. They slowed circled where she stood motionless.

"Not a good idea, weird mice," she growled.

They cackled, ignoring her warning.

The one on her right lunged, claws at the ready.

THWACK BAM POW SCRATCH

Annika sat, licking her paw, tail swishing in anger. The three weird horned mice lay in a huddle, claw marks all over them and large welts on their face.

"I told you it wasn't a good idea, stupid weird mice," she growled at them again.

The one she followed from the basement pouted as it rubbed one of its wounds.

"You aren't like the other one," it whined, "Why aren't you like the other one? He was fun."

Annika hissed and the thing scrambled under its fellow to hide from her glare.

"You were the ones who picked on my friend, then," she said. She went low to the ground, ready to pounce once more.

One of the other things put up its weird long hands.

"No, no, I mean, yes," it tried to smile, its face crooked, "but it wasn't our idea. We were only doing what the big guy told us to do."

Annika straightened up, striding closer to the trio.

"Take me to this big guy," she ordered.

They all nodded immediately, tripping onto their feet and bowing to her.

They led her away from the staircase, through a tunnel of dark rock.

On the other side the four of them emerged into almost a forest. Trees sprouted from the ground and shrubs wound around the trunks. However, the trees were made of dark, shining stone, and giant thorns covered the shrubs. Above the tops of the trees a swirling vortex filled the sky.

Annika didn't break stride, despite the strange surroundings. Honestly, it was hardly stranger than her home of gray cement and countless blocks of mushed up paper sheets.

The trio seemed put out when she didn't react to the strangeness of the forest, but they covered their disappointment by bowing to her over and over again as they weaved along the path through the trees. Eventually she had to whack them again to keep them from slowing her down.

Not that she didn't deserve such adoration, of course.

Farther and farther into the forest they travelled, until Annika got so bored with the walking that she actually began to pay attention to her surroundings. And because she paid attention, she saw the tunnel they had exited earlier through a gap in the trees. And when she saw the tunnel she spun around in alarm, and almost ran into the other three creatures sneaking up on her.

A few moments later, Annika stood up at her full height, fur at maximum fluff.

"You weird mice," she growled, "are going to take me to the Big Guy. Or. You will find out how I deal with regular, not weird, mice."

The six creatures sat on their now crooked tails and nursed a variety of new scratches on their arms and shoulders. She jumped forward a few inches and all six of them flinched away, scrambling to put the others creatures between them and Annika.

"I'll give you a hint," she hissed at the cowering forms, "missing tails are the least of their worries."

This time when they headed into the forest, Annika held six tails in her mouth like leashes. She would have to wash her mouth out about a million times, but it was the only way to keep the weird creatures in line. Two had tried to scamper off through the thorny underbrush already.

This time the forest changed quickly, the darkness falling heavier and the strange stone trees reaching farther into the sky. Tendrils of smoke reached down and shivered along the branches.

Then the trees vanished, and a huge throne of big fluffy pillows towered before them.

Queen Annika of the Goblins

Resting on the throne was a large…something. It was kind of furry, and kind of scaly, and really just rather gross. Annika imagined it was some kind of weird, ugly cat.

Weird Ugly Cat's eyes bugged out as their group of seven stumbled up to its feet.

Annika spit out the tails and batted the six creatures out of her way. She stomped up to the Weird Ugly Cat and snapped her jaws.

"You. Must be the Big Guy. You were mean to my best friend. And I don't like you."

She raised a paw when she finished, unsheathing her claws. The six smaller creatures screeched and ran to hide in nearby shrubbery.

The Big Guy/Weird Ugly Cat seemed to get the (correct) idea Annika was not just any cat. He shrank into himself, his eyes exploding like ping pongs balls from his head.

Then he paused for a moment and apparently remembered he was a big shot in whatever this place was. He puffed himself up and stared down his ugly nose at her.

"Nobody speaks to me like that," he croaked at her, "I am the King here!"

Annika flinched back for a heartbeat, her ears flattening against her head.

Then *she* remembered that she was Annika. And she was the greatest, most beautiful, most ferocious cat alive.

"I." She jumped up onto the throne.

"Don't." She slapped a clawed hand on the Big Guy's shoulder.

"Care."

Annika sat on the pillow throne, kneading the soft cushion beneath her.

Below the throne the six creatures cowered with the Big Guy, who now had countless scratch marks all over him.

"I think," Annika said, and the seven creatures below her groveled, "that we could think of something to make my friend Squeekie happy, don't you agree?"

They all nodded so fast their heads were a blur.

"Of course Queen Annika," they all blubbered together.

She preened.

"I could get used to this," she purred.

The sun peeked out and shone into the bookstore. Squeekie poked his head out of the cubby where he had spent all night hiding. He sniffed the air.

Annika had gone after the goblin things that bothered him, and she still wasn't back. He couldn't smell her, not a whiff.

He yowled softly, calling for her.

No response.

He whimpered and padded toward the back room, hoping she had fallen asleep somewhere and hadn't been captured by horrible goblin things.

He would go to save her, of course, but he wouldn't like it.

At the door he caught a fresh scent of Annika, his only warning before a horrible clattering rang out from the back room. Squeekie shot behind a bookcase to hide once more, trembling as he peered around the corner.

Four of the horrible goblin things carried a large platform, and perched on the top was a ball of fluff.

"Annika!" Squeekie cried, and shot out from his hiding place.

The creatures halted in front of Squeekie, and Annika smiled down at him.

"I have a surprise for you," she purred.

"Underlings," she called toward the back room.

Another group of goblin things rushed out, carrying a huge box. They set it before Squeekie and backed away, bowing the whole time.

Annika pounced from her seat and landed on the top of the box, upending it and spilling the contents out. Bundles and bundles of green leaves landed on the floor.

"Catnip!" she said, and then bowled Squeekie over with a huge hug.

"I'm still their queen," she told Squeekie later that day, after the store opened, and the catnip and the platform had been cleared away by her underlings, "but I think I'll let them be unless they get out of hand again. I'll stick around here and be a bookstore cat instead. After all, you'd be lost without me."

"I would," Squeekie agreed, "and I bet you would miss it."

Annika scoffed, and Squeekie batted her nose gently, and then the two of them chased each other through the aisles.

Squeekie was happy, and because Squeekie was happy, so was Annika.

Samantha Coons

AUTHOR BIOGRAPHY

Sometimes Annika lets **Samantha Coons** pet her, and Samantha is honored. Samantha also writes words sometimes and sometimes they are even good. She edited this book and wrote any text not attributed to another author. She would like you to know all mistakes in this book are her fault.

12

Peek-a-boo, Annik-a-boo

Carrie Jacobs

"Peek-a-boo! I see you!"

I opened my eyes to slits and glared at the one who dared disturb me. My withering glare was enough to frighten most, but not Steve. Probably because Steve was already dead. That's right, I'm tortured and disturbed by a stinking ghost. And I mean *stinking* literally. Every time Steve glides into a room, he brings with him the stench of wet dog.

If there's anything I hate more than being disturbed, it's dog. Foul, uncouth creatures, always slobbering and bouncing and more than happy to enjoy their enslavement to the humans. Fools.

"Peek-a-boo!" Steve knocked a book off the top shelf. It whizzed past my head and landed on the floor. "Annik-a-boo! I see you!"

I stood and stretched, then poured all the disdain I could muster into my stare. "How clever. You can rhyme."

Steve danced a jig in front of me, sticking his thumbs in his ears and wiggling his fingers. "Oooh," he mocked, "yooo kin rhyyyyme."

"I can also send you Away."

He snorted and tossed another book at me. I hissed, letting him know I was serious. I rarely had to send a ghost Away, but sometimes their behavior left me no choice. I trotted up the catwalk to the loft, making my rounds along the tops of the bookcases, surveying my domain.

"Peek-a-boo!" A book flew over the shelf in front of me.

"Stop messing up the books, Steve."

He mocked, "Stahp missig up duh burks, Stiv," then floated

away.

"Ignore him," Squeekie warned.

"I'm trying, but he's making a mess. It's making more work for the humans."

"I didn't know you cared."

I turned and looked at Squeekie. "When they have more work, they have less time. When they have less time, we get fewer treats."

"I suppose you have a point."

What a silly notion. Of *course* I had a point. "And when they find books all over the floor, they think it's one of us."

I had him there. Sweet, lovable, silly Squeekie. Always willing to give the benefit of the doubt, but even he didn't like people who messed with his favorite humans. Living *or* dead. I waited until the stench wafted away and I knew Steve was out of hearing range. "I'm sending him Away."

"Oh, Annika, that should only be a last resort. He's a brand new ghost. I'll try talking to him. Maybe he'll be a good friend in the long run."

I doubted it, but as usual, I let Squeekie talk me out of sending Steve Away. He was right. New ghosts were exponentially more insufferable than ghosts who'd been at it for a while.

For a few weeks, nothing much changed. Steve would jump out of one of the shelves, hurl books at me and scream, "Peek-a-boo!"

Then, one day, it all changed.

I was doing my rounds atop the bookshelves when I found a pile of books, carefully arranged into a square, with a large book on top. Inside the makeshift box, something mewed. I carefully wiggled and shifted the book on top, only to find that Steve had trapped one of the rescue kittens!

The kitten sniffled and I told her to go to the kitty condo and take a nap. Then I went to find Squeekie.

I searched all over the bookstore, but Squeekie was nowhere to be found. The fur on the back of my neck stood up, not that you could tell. I searched some more, and had almost given up when I spotted a paintbrush on the floor in front of a small closet.

This wasn't right at all. Squeekie took his paintbrushes to the

Peek-a-boo, Annik-a-boo

humans. He didn't leave them on the floor, all willy-nilly.

The closet door had been wedged shut with an old encyclopedia. I nudged the heavy tome aside and put my paw under the corner of the door, jerking it to and fro until it popped open.

Squeekie burst out, cobwebs and dust bunnies stuck to his fur. He shook them off. "Thanks, Neek, it was scary in there!"

Oh, *heck* no.

Squeekie and I went back to the store to check on the three rescue kitties. When they were accounted for, Steve sent a new book by a local author sailing at me. I ducked while he cackled, "Peek-a-boo!"

The book – a *new* book! – hit the shelf and fell to the floor, several of its pages getting bent in the process.

Enough was enough. All books were to be treated with respect, but *especially* the new ones.

"Peek-a-boo!" Steve popped his transparent head through one of the shelves and tried to scare me.

Ignoring him, I gracefully padded to the back room. Casting a glance around, I made sure no one was watching me – living or dead – before I slunk down the stairs to the cold basement.

George the Ghost made an unpleasant noise. "What brings you down here?"

I crinkled my beautiful flat nose and managed to hold back a sarcastic remark. The very tip of my floofy tail flicked with annoyance. I didn't like being questioned. I didn't like ghosts. I *certainly* did not like being questioned by a ghost. "I have a ghost I need to send Away."

You wouldn't think a ghost could go pale, but they can. George certainly did. "Not me, right?" He gulped.

I waved a paw, dismissing his stupidity. "Are you Away?"

"No…"

"Then I obviously don't want to send you there. Got it?"

George's attitude always significantly improved after reminding him what I was capable of. "How may I assist you?"

"Get me the key."

"Yes, Annika, right away." George floated into the darkness and came back a moment later. He dropped the aged silver skeleton key at my feet and eyed it warily.

I hid the key into my fur and made my way back upstairs. I couldn't wait to groom the stench of basement off my feet.

But that would have to wait.

"Peek-a-boo!"

I ducked, but nothing came at me. No, Steve had cornered the three rescue kittens *and* Squeekie in the kitty condo. The kittens cried as books banged against the metal bars. Squeekie shielded them and hissed.

Wait. Squeekie hissed?

I nearly froze in shock, then anger consumed me. I darted to the section of the bookstore that housed the antique books. There was a small cabinet there that no one could open. Not without the key.

I jammed the key into the lock and turned it. The loud click was drowned out by that idiot Steve shrieking, "Peek-a-boo!" again.

I dragged a small box out of the cabinet. The only adornment on the box was the word "Away" carved into it. Its magic vibrated against my paws as I carefully placed it on the yellow brick road.

Steve saw me and tossed a book. "Peek-a-boo!"

I hooked one claw into the ancient wooden box and unlocked the lid.

Steve flew back and forth over the kitty condo, yelling and banging to scare the kittens.

"Why don't you pick on someone your own size?" I taunted.

He stopped and darted back the aisle.

I smelled his nasty wet dog smell as he came down the next aisle. A book scraped against the shelf as he pulled it out.

The box in front of me pulsated with a magical force.

The book whizzed past my head.

Steve laughed and cackled, "Peek-a-boo!"

I flicked the box open. Its magic began pulling Steve toward it. He yelled and hollered and grabbed at the shelves, knocking over books and tearing pages.

As the box sucked him in, sending him Away, I said, "No, Steve. *Annik-a*-boo."

Peek-a-boo, Annik-a-boo

AUTHOR BIOGRAPHY

Carrie Jacobs began her writing career at age three, when, still lacking the dexterity to form recognizable letters, she dictated a riveting tale to her transcriptionist, AKA Mom. "A Frog Named Tog" rocketed to #1 in the family, but did not garner international acclaim. It did, however, serve as an early clue that writing would be a lifelong journey.

Since then, she spent approximately fifteen years as a columnist for a local weekly newspaper, writing "slice of life" type articles. She also frequently write articles for a local non-profit. Carrie has won two first-place awards through Pennwriters.

She loves writing contemporary romance novels, and writes short stories in any genre imaginable, including the weird and creepy. Her settings are many places she's visited and her hometown, all thrown into a blender and poured out into the place she would most love to live. Her characters are people she knows, would like to know, or would like to avoid.

Carrie lives in beautiful central Pennsylvania with her family and spoiled pets.

Connect with her on Facebook at facebook.com/writercarriejacobs, on Twitter at @carrieinpa or on her website at carrieajacobs.com.

Annika the Reluctant Bookstore Cat

The Very, Very Bad Misadventures of
Annika the Reluctant Bookstore Cat

Content Warning for Story 13

WARNING!

DO NOT READ TO CHILDREN

RATED B & V

FOR **BLOOD** & **VIOLENCE**

(SERIOUSLY)

DO NOT READ TO CHILDREN

Annika the Reluctant Bookstore Cat

13

Of Mice and Murder

Odessa Moon

Annika had always enjoyed being a cat. She knew her place in the universe and this life, unlike some of her previous lives, suited her very well. She was warm, safe, fed, out of the weather, she exercised her talents on a daily basis, and she had company when she felt like acknowledging the presence of others.

Lately, however, she suffered from a surfeit of company. They followed her everywhere; a murmuring, resentful ghostly horde always nipping at her heels and reaching with spectral paws to clutch at her tail. It was annoying. Their moans and whispers were even more irritating as they disturbed her nap schedule and distracted her from her duties as a bookstore cat.

The horde of ghost mice had become more insistent, possibly because she kept adding new members to their ranks. Hunting was a pleasure she indulged in as often as possible, a pleasure highlighted by the kill. She patiently stalked her victims, learning their deceitful habits and destructive ways, how they squirmed their way under the shelves and found new paths via the HVAC system to skulk unseen. Annika loved sinking her fangs into the neck of a mouse, feeling the gush of hot, warm blood flooding her mouth and the snap of the neck. The sensation of life abandoning a body made her day, every day. Nibbling on their tiny feet, picking her teeth with the bones, and then leaving the corpses artistically arranged for Michelle to find rounded out the experience.

It was always fun to watch Michelle discover a mouse by stepping on it.

However, the ever-growing horde of ghost mice was getting to her. They accused her of murder. Her wanton slaughter, so they whispered, destroyed families that had lived for generations inside the bookstore. Did not the mice too have a right to healthy, happy lives? Lives they lived out, nibbling on the delicious paper and glue contained within the books? Who wanted those old heaps of paper anyway? The mice were doing the bookstore a favor by chewing up the unwanted volumes into snug nests for their children. So they said, over and over, whispering to her endlessly in the night.

The ghost mice began invading her dreams. She was restless. Unhappy. The universe was not what it should be. Annika could feel her confidence in herself eroding away. Each kill was becoming harder.

The mice accused her with their beady eyes when she pinned them to the floor, her claws delicately splayed across their thrashing bodies, a ruby drop at each tip. It was irritating, listening to their shrill squeaks for dead family members when she snapped their necks. Why couldn't they shut up and accept their fate? She was doing them a favor, helping them to rejoin those dead and gone relatives in the afterlife.

Annika lay in a pool of sunlight. She normally relished the life-giving rays that soaked into her bones and warmed her fur, but no longer. She fretted as she groomed herself, patiently going over each whisker and licking the blood from her claws.

What was a cat for if not to slaughter vermin?

The other cats were no help with her dilemma. Squeekie was a sycophant, dispensing his favors indiscriminately to anyone who came near him. He had no pride. He barely bothered to notice the mice, a most un-catlike behavior.

The rotating parade of visiting cats was worse. They purred and frolicked and played the fool in a constant plea for attention and adoption from bookstore customers. As if any place could be better than the bookstore. Why did they want to leave? She didn't. They weren't much better mousers than that bootlicking Squeekie.

Yet those idiotic cats, incompetent mousers all, were happy. They were happier than she was.

Of Mice and Murder

Perhaps, Annika mused, she was, well, not wrong, precisely. She could never be wrong. But it was possible there was something to their foolish philosophy. It was working. She was a practical, observant cat and that was a practical consideration. Those cats were contented and happy whereas she was not.

She could try out their lifestyle.

So she did.

Annika made every effort to purr fetchingly. She allowed grubby hands to stroke her beautiful fur. She tolerated cooing about her cuteness since it was fully justified. She made a determined effort to be friendlier with bookstore customers as well as the staff. She ignored their comments that maybe there was something wrong with her, and she needed to see the vet.

Hours went by, days went by, weeks went by. The immense effort of imitating a winsome and adorable kitty consumed all her energy so she stopped slaughtering mice.

When she was honest with herself, she was still unhappy, but this time in a different way. It felt so wrong, yet the results couldn't be denied. The customers and the bookstore staff fell all over themselves petting her and playing with her and adoring her. As they should!

To her surprise, the horde of ghost mice became quieter, also an improvement. They stopped haunting her dreams. They began to fade away, one by one, their spectral paws no longer clutching at her tail.

The live mice, on the other hand, slowly became more annoying. She did her best to ignore them, like the other cats did. The mice didn't taunt her like the ghost mice had. They didn't dare. Too many of them remembered generations of dead relatives. They pretended she didn't exist. They skittered around the bookstore, leaving their droppings everywhere. They chewed on the books, leaving shredded paper in corners.

And they bred. Oh, how they bred. New generation after new generation of mice, each larger than the last. They were running wild. And then, worse, Annika realized the mouse population of the bookstore wasn't growing just because the mice were reproducing, unchecked by regular culling of the mischief*. (FOOTNOTE: Living in a bookstore was educational so Annika knew the correct collective noun for mice. She thought 'mischief' was a good word because it described them so well.)

The mice had become bold enough to invite outside mice to move into the bookstore. These new mice were openly disrespectful to her. They were disrespectful to the other cats as well, but that was unimportant.

More and more books were damaged. Michelle and the staff began to notice – it certainly had taken them long enough – and complain. The other cats remained mostly useless.

Then, as Annika lay stretched out in a puddle of moonlight, exhausted from the effort of being personable all day, it happened. A mouse ran across her tail. Then another one, followed by yet another.

They were treating her like a stuffed toy! As though she was made of velveteen and sawdust. As though she wasn't a cat at all.

Annika lay there, horrified. She had become a toy cat and not a real one. She no longer knew what she was. She laid in the puddle of moonlight while the mischief of mice frolicked around her as though she wasn't there at all.

As though she didn't exist.

Was she still a cat?

What was a cat?

Annika forced herself to think, doing her best to ignore the skitter of paws across her long tail and the shrill, disrespectful squeaks filling the air. She let memories of other lives flood over her, remembering.

A cat was a hunter. A cat was death on silent paws. A cat was an apex predator, scourge of all she surveyed. A cat was a killing machine, perfectly designed by nature to slaughter small, squeaky creatures. A cat was proud of the honor guard of ghost mice who followed her around, demonstrating to all the other cats her hunting prowess.

Was she still a cat? Annika leaped to her paws, galvanized by her new understanding. She *was* a cat, the perfect cat, the textbook example of what a cat should be, and it was time to do something about the mice.

Of Mice and Murder

The slaughter was intense.

The aisles of the bookstore ran with blood. Her horde of ghost mice returned and their ranks doubled, then doubled again. It was glorious. How she had missed the taste of blood, the smell of death, the sensation of doing exactly what brain and body were designed for.

She was a cat, a hunting cat, and she was proud of it. The horde of ghost mice were not haunting her. Their presence honored her and she did not have to listen to their mealy-mouthed complaints.

They were mice! They deserved a snap of the neck and a slow disembowelment. The books would be safe again.

It was a long, long night but dawn came at last. Annika spent first light arranging many of her kills into rows by the front door. The rest she left where they fell, intestines and blood smeared on the floor around the corpse.

Then she went to a comfortable spot nearby and settled into a good grooming session followed by a well-deserved nap. Annika knew what would come next and she wanted to be well-rested for the occasion. It would be amusing.

She woke up to the sound of the key in the lock, followed by Michelle's first footstep into the bookstore.

Then Michelle's screams.

It *was* amusing, and welcome too after such a long time of not hearing it. And better, she'd be hearing Michelle's periodic scream along with the rest of the staff for the entire day as they discovered all the dead mice she had left strewn about.

Annika yawned hugely and resumed cleaning her claws. It had been a good night and she was already looking forward to the evening.

She knew who she was now. She was not just Annika, the bookstore cat. She was Annika, the scourge of heaven, and she would not forget again.

Odessa Moon

AUTHOR BIOGRAPHY

Odessa Moon has at various times painted, sewed, served in the Navy, worked as a sales clerk and cashier, taken care of her family, and gardened with enthusiasm. She reads extensively, especially on subjects like medieval history, the class struggle, colonization, and resource depletion. While growing up, she read piles of science-fiction and fantasy and often wondered what the authors hand-waved away about how difficult it really would be to terraform another planet. The series, "The Steppes of Mars" is her attempt to combine all those interests.

When Ms. Moon is not writing, she is working on improving the soil in her own garden and planting trees in her municipality.

*The Very, Very Bad Misadventures of
Annika the Reluctant Bookstore Cat*

ABOUT THE AUTHOR

Annika is the reluctant bookstore cat at The Cupboard Maker Books in Enola, Pennsylvania. She loves treats, and she tolerates her best friend Squeekie the bookstore cat. If you are very lucky she will let you pet her without injury. Annika and Squeekie have helped find over 130 Castaway Critters their Furever homes.

www.ingramcontent.com/pod-product-compliance
Lightning Source LLC
Chambersburg PA
CBHW071007080526
44587CB00015B/2375